MW00356115

Unstuck

How to Unlock and Activate
the Wisdom of Others

Craig Lemasters

To learn more about this book and its author, please visit
www.craiglemasters.com

Copyright © 2020 by Craig Lemasters
All Rights Reserved
ISBN: 978-1-64180-072-3
Version 1.0

Cover design and illustration by Rick Nease
www.RickNeaseArt.com

Published By
Front Edge Publishing, LLC
42807 Ford Road
Canton, MI

Front Edge Publishing books are available for discount bulk purchases
for events, corporate use and small groups. Special editions, including
books with corporate logos, personalized covers and customized
interiors are available for purchase. For more information, contact
Front Edge Publishing at info@FrontEdgePublishing.com

This book is dedicated to everyone who feels stuck.

Contents

Introduction by Rita J. King ·   1

PART 1: STUCK

Disruption ·   9
You're Not Alone ·   13
Are You Stuck? ·   24
The Missing Link ·   34

PART 2: UNSTUCK

Get Humble ·   44
Draw the Destination ·   50
Smart People Ask for What They Need · · · · · · · · · · · · · · · ·   62
'Thinking Outside the Building' ·   72
Make It Happen ·   84
A Question of Vocation ·   95

Now what? ·   104
About the Author ·   105
Resources ·   106

Praise for *Unstuck*

Few things, besides your values and mission, remain unchanged as you grow from any early stage business to a late stage company. In parallel, leaders need to grow and evolve to navigate the journey. Having been through it numerous times, and helped other companies scale as well, I have experienced the merits and drawbacks of various leadership paradigms. The method Craig lays out in this book is one way of meeting that challenge.

What I love about Craig's approach is how it brings the collective experience of a group of leaders to bear on a specific growth challenge. Too often, companies plan incessantly with limited action, and their leaders often fall victim to omission bias and loss aversion, thereby stunting growth and a performance culture. As an external advisor, I help them take a step forward toward actually doing something—to get comfortable with discomfort. It's a compelling way to solve business challenges while also engaging the group's curiosity. I'd recommend the *Unstuck* way of working to anyone interested in making meaningful connections while getting things done.

Dinesh Moorjani
Managing Director, Comcast Ventures

It's hard to describe the feeling of reading a story that you lived through, told from someone else's perspective. But Craig accurately captures a lot of how it felt to face these challenges, highs and lows. It was brilliant to share the room with people who sincerely wanted to help us learn. I encourage any leader to try the principles of *Unstuck*—I think you'll be surprised by the rigor, creativity and even fun you can have in these kinds of conversations. Craig's approach is something I've been glad to carry forward in my work life.

Stephen Ebbett
Chief Digital and Marketing Officer at American Addiction Centers

Craig's *Unstuck* methodology accelerates learning to help you break through tough business challenges like a champ. By drawing on the wisdom of those who have walked the path before you, his approach gets you desired results with years of experience packed in only a few short sessions.

Michelle Weese
General Secretary, Danone North America

Wisdom-based learning is a leader's secret weapon, allowing them to act quickly and with confidence. I've seen the impact of this model firsthand as an advisor and was blown away by the results we were able to help the organization achieve after just a few quick meetings. The message of this book is "spot on" for these times!

John Featherston
Senior Director, New Ventures, Chick-fil-A

Introduction

The group moved together up the spiral staircase, joking nervously about all the steps ahead of them. Some of them were out of breath, others were excited. Some stopped to look at the art as they went up, floor by floor, through a Manhattan townhouse where Abraham Lincoln's granddaughter lived for 35 years. Now it's the headquarters for Science House, the company I co-direct. The building is extremely vertical. It's a cathedral of imagination, designed to be a place where people can relax, focus, and think.

Our clients include many different companies across industries who often come to immerse themselves in the Imagination Room, filling the walls with diagrams, words, pictures, and ideas.

On this particular day, the leader of the group was Craig Lemasters, then CEO of Assurant Solutions. After realizing Assurant lagged when it came to digital development, Craig had made some bold assertions about the company's future transformation and revenue goals. His words inspired his direct reports and the entire company, but, as you might imagine from your own experience, reality immediately set in. He didn't know where to start, and everyone was looking to him for answers. He started having meetings at Assurant.

"Stuck companies tend to have lots of meetings," Craig notes, "with lots of people, that lead to very little output. Surely if you just put enough brains together ..."

Our specialty at Science House is applying the scientific method to bringing clarity and purpose to meetings. I can picture, as I'm sure you can, what these meetings must have been like. Even the smartest people who are stuck will spin their wheels without getting very far. And meetings, after all, aren't just about getting people in a room. They reveal the very essence of business and shared purpose.

Realizing that he needed to try something else, Craig brought his team to Science House to meet with us and an advisory board assembled by a consultancy called GXG. Finally, they made it all the way upstairs and took their seats. I was impressed when Craig set the tone for a day of listening by admitting that the purpose for the session was to get unstuck.

We all get stuck. There's no shame in that. The problem starts when we refuse to do anything about it. Leading organizations during this unprecedented time in human history is not an easy task.

At the beginning of my career I was a journalist. I researched and wrote about systems, such as the relationship between corporations and the government, the digital culture and the nuclear industry. In 2006, IBM engaged me as a consultant to investigate the business value of the company's emerging digital culture. After years of studying corporate culture from the outside, I found myself advising senior executives from within. The world became increasingly interconnected, though what we've seen so far is nothing compared to what's ahead. The iPhone was invented, but nobody knew yet how much that small rectangle in our pockets would change us irrevocably for better and worse, or how much reach it would have.

Over time, in working with senior executives across industries, I realized they were stuck between the Industrial Era and the Intelligence Era. Products created in the Industrial Era are tangible and heavy. These tend to be objects that our brains can understand. People putting a car together might not be able to design one, but they know one when they see it and can connect their contribution to the end result. The Industrial Era isn't in its zenith, but it isn't behind us, either. At the height of the revolution, captains of industry wanted conveyor belts moving faster and faster. Amazon's warehouse workers are measured and monitored in the same way, turned into living robots until mechanical counterparts have hands capable of grasping, holding and moving parcels of different sizes.

As we move into the Intelligence Era, the impulse for greater speed doesn't make sense even as companies try to do more and more with less. This idea seems counterintuitive. Of course we *have* to move quickly, right? No. Speed isn't the real problem. You can move very quickly in the wrong direction and waste time, energy, and money doing it. Leaders of the lingering juggernauts find themselves in a tough position trying to update a tangle of outdated spaghetti code, move to the cloud, modernize their software architecture, development and design practices. They grapple with rigid, hierarchical org charts topped by executives who became successful at a different time. They struggle to keep pace with constantly changing customer demands. Analytical skills are now in high demand on the business side, and information technology groups now need to learn the art and science of clear, concise communication to breathe life into the art of the possible.

Intelligence Era work products can be nebulous and are often invisibly woven into society. Workers who need to focus and think their way through complicated challenges with hazy boundaries are instead often forced to react to new emergencies. It's difficult to recognize and prioritize core essentials when everything feels like a burning platform. Knowledge workers can work from anywhere, making it harder to get time to recharge.

I started to think about the transition time in between these two eras as the Imagination Age. The main skill is AI. These letters shouldn't stand for artificial intelligence, a term that tends to get thrown around loosely to mean many things. AI is applied imagination. It takes imagination to identify the right problems to solve. It takes imagination to look at an abundance of data and find valuable insights within it, not just to sell more things to more people, but to improve the quality of our lives. We think of imagination as a whimsical part of childhood, but it's a human superpower. It starts developing immediately, and over time we clamp it down and hold it back as we attempt to carve out a professional and personal path in life. Instead, we should develop it even more, practice it as a rigorous discipline, and use it to shape a version of the future worth inhabiting.

The business landscape has changed along with the fields of Silicon Valley, once home to apricot orchards. The challenges faced by most senior executives now didn't exist back when they took their first professional positions on the long road up the org chart. It's scary to look down from that authoritative vantage point and wonder what everyone is going to think when you admit that you're stuck. But it's inevitable, at some point, and there are people out there who can help you because they've been where you are now and they've navigated a path forward through the ambiguity.

At the end of Assurant's successful transformation, Craig left and bought GXG. He infused the company's model with the experience of his own process, intellectual and emotional honesty to overcome inevitable defense mechanisms, and the part I like best—meaningful conversations with people who have been there and just want to help. Staying stuck for too long can be an existential threat for a company or an individual. Craig understands the feeling of being in charge and being terrified at the same time. His model at GXG discreetly fills the knowledge gaps that we all have so we don't stay stuck in them. This is achieved with one-on-one conversations with people Craig calls operators who have faced similar challenges, whatever they may be, from software architecture to understanding new markets to figuring out how to operationalize a bold idea.

This model is extremely powerful. It speaks to me on a deep level because I have a lifelong passion for collaborative, creative pairs. My life and work are arranged around this principle. The importance of two people connecting around a purpose drives progress in a way that nothing else can. In groups, politics and bureaucracy tend to dominate. In pairs, the energy and focus is pure. Pairs give and take in unique ways to learn from each other. A creative pair is a dance of ideas. Pairs exchange knowledge and learn. There's nowhere to hide in a pair. In these moments of sharing, vulnerability and listening, we open a portal into an improved version of ourselves.

When I hear Craig describe his journey as a CEO, through 44 quarters including peaks, valleys and plateaus, I'm struck by the way it resembles the formula for a great, gripping story in which a person faces many trials and tribulations, including a dark night of the soul, in order to persevere in the epic battle to gain wisdom. There's a reason a story like this is called a page turner. As readers, we want to see what kind of challenges the protagonist is going to face. We ask ourselves what we would do in such a situation.

At the beginning of every great story is an ordinary person who is inclined to resist the invitation for an extraordinary adventure because it's overwhelming to imagine everything that comes next. What makes the protagonist extraordinary isn't that he or she never fails, but that they are willing to try, to learn, to allow a mentor to illuminate new angles of thinking, being and doing. Nothing great is accomplished alone. We all get stuck sometimes, and we all have the capacity to get unstuck and move forward with help from those who have faced the same crossroads. I've seen Craig when he's stuck, and I've seen him get unstuck. I've been a witness to his own development throughout the journey described in this book. You're in good company.

As a final note, this introduction was written prior to the pandemic that forced us into isolation and required us to find new ways to work together. Unstuck, however, was not yet published, so I reviewed the introduction to see if it might be outdated in light of the new reality we face. In the end, I didn't change a word, but I will add this. In the past month I have seen clients finally make strides toward the future state they imagined for a long time. In the absence of a catalyzing event, it is difficult to make systemic change. My hope is that as we recover from this time, we place new emphasis on improving the systems that govern our lives. Individuals are often stuck within these systems, so learning how to get unstuck also includes collaborating on the creation of a world worth inhabiting now and in the future.

—Rita J. King

Rita is a futurist who works with senior leadership teams around the world to take ideas from mind to market and design organizations that can get things done. She has served as Innovator-in-Residence at IBM and futurist at NASA Langley's think-tank. Rita is currently a futurist at the Science and Entertainment Exchange of the National Academy of Sciences, for which she invents technologies, novel characters and story architecture.

W = K x E

Wisdom equals knowledge multiplied by experience.

I know kicking off my book with an equation can seem a little uninviting to a general audience. But I think the simplicity of this equation communicates a great deal and I wanted to give it to you upfront.

Here is the punchline: the further away from our core business we must move, whether by choice or under external pressure, the more likely we are to get stuck. I believe the only way to get unstuck in time for our companies to not just survive, but thrive after change, is to identify and inject the wisdom we're missing. Wisdom that is the product of specific knowledge and hands-on experience solving problems like the ones we're facing.

If you're sold and you can't wait to learn how this works, go ahead and skip to Part 2. I'm ready to guide you on the Unstuck journey. If you're skeptical, curious to see me make my case, or want to dive into why stuck happens in the first place, turn the page. Because behind every equation is a story. This is mine.

Part 1: Stuck

Disruption

Stories like the one I'm about to tell you, of disruption and accelerating change, are so familiar by now that it's difficult to describe the business environment without sounding cliché. Quantified, however, it still retains some of its punch: As Barry Ritholtz pointed out for IndustryWeek, the landline telephone took 75 years to reach 50 million users. That milestone was achieved by airplanes in 68 years, the automobile in 62 years, lightbulbs in 46 years, and television in 22 years. YouTube, Facebook, Twitter, and the Angry Birds app reached 50 million users in four years, three years, two years, and 35 days, respectively.[1]

In other words, for most of human history on this planet, change has consistently been gradual. Only in the most recent three decades of civilization has change accelerated so rapidly that it poses a formidable challenge to the acquisition of *timely* knowledge, let alone accumulating the depth and range of knowledge needed to get ahead of change. My goal, and my full-time vocation, is to meet leaders in that moment of stuck and share a way to get unstuck.

In 1987, I joined American Bankers Insurance Group, a company that would become a part of Assurant, a global insurance company. In

---

1 https://www.industryweek.com/technology/
world-about-undergo-even-faster-change

2000, I moved to the Atlanta-based division, Assurant Solutions and in 2005 became CEO. We specialized in a niche called credit insurance. These particular policies assured people taking out major loans that their debts would be paid off in case of a catastrophe. At the time, that was a $2 billion business, but major changes in the financial sector soon made it clear to me that credit insurance was a dying industry. I could see that particular product was out of favor and was certain to fade.

That did not mean our company was destined to fail. After all, we were more than one particular product. As a solid business-to-business (B2B) insurer, our core capabilities were product development, actuarial pricing, processing claims, point of sale marketing, and inbound customer service. We were actually really good at several things! I knew that these capabilities could be adapted to other products.

In the early 2000s, the whole world was struggling through a turbulent era of change in consumer demand. Entirely new lines of consumer goods were appearing—personal computers, tablets, digital music devices, smart phones—and seemingly overnight these new devices were becoming essential to millions of men and women. Consumer expectations regarding customer service were also changing dramatically. A new era of immediacy was starting to emerge. But it was the smartphone in particular that was becoming the real game changer.

This gave me a lot to think about as a leader. Our core product was under attack and customer expectations were rising. A daunting combination!

Can We Morph?

So we made that first crucial decision to morph our product line from credit insurance to products (extended service contracts) that protected the long list of consumer products flowing into homes around the world. We built upon the same core capabilities that had carried us this far. Our previously acquired expertise was opening a broad new horizon for us as a strong provider of service contracts. After several years of hard work and perseverance, we became the leaders at providing such contracts to brown-and-white retailers, the industry phrase for big-ticket merchandise that traditionally came in brown and white:

refrigerators, stoves, washers, driers, and stereos, back when stereos came in big brown boxes. Each year heralded a new influx of devices. The iPhone and Kindle arrived in 2007. A host of other electronic devices, from computers to high-tech vacuum cleaners—and from kitchen appliances to gizmos for the car—were rolling into big-box stores. We soon built a thriving business providing those retailers with the extended service contracts that reassured customers.

The problem was that the digital revolution was making those stores obsolete. I had to brace myself before opening the business section of my newspaper each morning. More than once, I found an unpleasant surprise. I will never forget David Pogue's 2007 technology column in *The New York Times*, headlined: "The Gutting of CompUSA." Pogue wrote: "I think the real culprit behind the gutting of CompUSA is Internet pricing. You can order computers, accessories and electronics from the Web for a fraction of CompUSA's in-store prices—and evidently, most people are doing exactly that."

With the news of CompUSA's crash, I was more than frustrated. That meant we were losing hundreds of millions of dollars of revenue from service contracts sold in those stores essentially overnight. How could we replace such a loss? No new chains of big-box stores were sprouting to replace the dinosaurs.

Digital Imperative

We already had dared to morph the company in one major new direction—expanding from credit insurance into the entirely new realm of extended service contracts for consumer products. That risk had paid off handsomely. The company was not only going to survive the downturn in credit insurance—it was booming with new business. But it didn't change the fact that the industry we were betting on was struggling, largely due to the acceleration of this "digital." Something I and my senior team didn't know a lot about. Clearly, we needed to morph the company yet again. The question was—actually I had a lot of questions—morph into what? How do we start? And here I was again—stuck!

I'm sharing my story in hopes that you'll recognize yourself or your company in my journey to getting unstuck, because I truly believe the process I bumped into all those years ago is the key to helping you. Because every organization, even the great ones, get stuck. It's the nature of the disruptive business environment we're in. The further we move away from our core business, driven by accelerating change, the less applicable our hard-earned knowledge and experience is to the realm of new things. It's always been this way.

You're Not Alone

If you're stuck—you're not alone.

In fact, if you don't think you're stuck on something right now, then you're probably kidding yourself. We all get stuck. Stuck is sneaky, because it's very rarely a complete standstill. Here are just a few of the descriptions I've heard from leaders in recent years of what it feels like:

"It feels like my senior leadership team doesn't want us to succeed! I mean, of course, I know that's not true. We all want to succeed. They're just terrified and are throwing up all kinds of excuses. What I'm facing from my own top people often feels harder than what we're facing out there in the world."

"It feels like I'm trying to walk in ankle-deep mud. I pull one foot out of the muck—and the other one slides even deeper. Then, I manage to pull that one free—and the first one now is up to my knee."

"At the very moment we're trying to summon the collective energy to bust into this tough new market, I'm drowning in a million emails. I just feel like locking my door and curling up in a corner."

"Our consultants keep describing new adjacencies, markets, geographies, etc. Sounds and looks simple on paper. Why is it so hard to get any momentum?"

In other words, if you're not making progress at the speed you want to be, if your day-to-day work is a flurry of activity without a lot of impact to show for it, you're definitely stuck. And you're probably miserable. I've been there and so have 99% of the leaders I've talked to.

Expectations: Literally Unrealistic

Stuck starts with a set of completely unrealistic expectations. Here is a picture I like to draw.

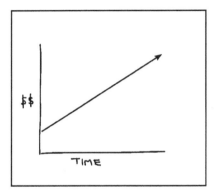

I call this the Expectation Line. What's so intimidating about this line? Every quarter, quarter after quarter, this is the way companies are measured today. Organizations and their leaders are held accountable for perfectly linear, steep, upward growth. Easy!

Public companies, private companies, big or small; I've drawn this picture for hundreds of executives and everyone generally agrees that this is what companies strive towards and are actually expected to produce. It's the natural extension of Milton Friedman's economic theories from the 1970s and the idea of shareholder primacy—that is, that the primary goal of a corporation is to create shareholder wealth. In fact, I typically describe my tenure as CEO not in years, but in quarters—about 44 in my case—and each capped with the question "What are you doing for me next quarter?"

As Sebastian Buck recently wrote for Fast Company, "One of the many problems with this theory is that shareholder primacy creates a completely blinkered view of the world: Leaders' attention is trained on one thing. This ignores the reality of the complex, living, evolving ecosystem in which corporations operate: a vast system of cause and effect. Managing for one short-term metric in a complex ecosystem inevitably results in unintended—or actively ignored—consequences […]" Nevertheless, the cycles keep churning and the Expectation Line accepts no excuses. There is no "Yeah, but … "

So of course the reality of what we're able to achieve is different.

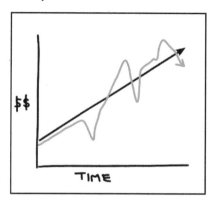

The red line is the reality most leaders face: a difficult journey through peaks, troughs, and plateaus. In fact, the red line is much closer to my line as CEO. At some point, like I found at Assurant, the growth in your core business won't be enough. You'll have to start branching out into new stuff, or adjacencies, as the traditional consulting firms call it, and that's super hard! But the Expectation Line assumes that companies can just double down at what they are good at and repeat success. The Expectation Line doesn't recognize that, in fact, we might simply lack the knowledge and experience we need to move successfully into a new space.

That's what creates this horrible feeling of stuck. When stakeholders narrowly focus on that expectation of growth one quarter at a time, getting stuck hurts. Staying stuck can be disastrous.

As leaders, we are forever getting stuck because we simply assume that all the wealth and resources at our command will inevitably prevail against whatever new forces might come at us. But the truth is when we get comfortable with the status quo, we stop tuning into the world around us and often miss a number of warning signs of the disruption to come.

Stuck then Struck

Usually, we get stuck because we can't seem to move fast enough. It's not that we aren't trying. It's not that we don't care. It's not that we don't have the work ethic. It just gets harder to move fast as we venture further outside our core.

Malcolm Gladwell zeroes in on this problem in his book, *David and Goliath*. For thousands of years, people have told that title story as if little David had almost no chance of surviving his battle with the gigantic Goliath. Gladwell retells the story with a different focus: Goliath was far too slow. Gladwell lays out a wealth of fascinating historical research and forensic science to explain that Goliath was actually was stuck. Goliath was relying on more than 100 pounds of weaponry designed for old-fashioned close combat. Instead, David was an agile young expert with a sling that modern ballistics experts say delivered the stopping power and accuracy of a modern .45-caliber handgun. Even as Goliath hollered across the field at David, Gladwell says he realized that he was stuck. And then? He was struck dead by the speed and precision of that one little stone with the deadly force of a bullet.

I certainly felt the devastating force of change in my CEO's chair, as I described in the previous chapter. What's most humbling for us in such situations? Remembering that we became leaders in the first place because we were the innovators! At Assurant, we owned our original niche in credit insurance, then we pulled off a startling, worldwide morphing of our company into a new line of products: service contracts for consumer goods. We were the visionaries—the winning team. We were the little guys with the potent weapons—the fresh ideas that would change the world. We were the Davids packing strategic power with pinpoint accuracy.

Until we weren't.

Our problem: Even though we had clarity of vision about our core business, we weren't talking to the right people about how to position the company for the digital future. We were locked into business practices that were not sustainable for next-generation growth.

I'm telling you our story because it's more than the story of Assurant Solutions. It's the story of American business. In fact, it's the story of international commerce.

From Cinema to Selfie

Thomas Edison didn't invent the first movie camera, but his staff did invent the first practical model of a movie camera for large-scale production in 1891. Edison was a master of patenting to control all of the new businesses he was launching. So, how did he let the French Lumière brothers invent the first successful movie projector several years later? After the camera, wasn't a projector the next logical product to design and patent? Instead, Edison let his team lose control of the movie industry at the very moment they were creating it.

One reason was that the Kinetograph camera was bulkier than the cameras that very quickly were designed and built in Europe in that era. As a result of their equipment's unwieldy size, Edison's movie crews shot their films while locked inside a small studio about the size of a house. The French were far more agile and began taking their cameras to public places that might surprise moviegoers. The Lumières made a world-famous movie of an actual train arriving at a station. That short film was so startling to first-time moviegoers that many people jumped from their seats in alarm! Edison's talent ran deep—but his team wasn't nimble in the movie industry.

For all their genius, Edison's wizards also failed to come up with the celluloid film that was essential if movie cameras were to become practical. That breakthrough in film technology came from George Eastman's Kodak company, another now-legendary center of American innovation.

Kodak's basic business model is replicated to this day. They controlled a vast catalog of patents, which locked in their exclusive right to manufacture and sell their entire product line. Then, they inexpensively priced their equipment—Kodak cameras—and made their recurring revenue on the necessary supplies: film, paper, and developing chemicals. For the better part of a century, George Eastman's business model was a juggernaut. By the mid-1970s, Kodak controlled 90% of film sales and 85% of camera sales in the U.S.

Why was Kodak so good at selling that first camera to a customer? The backbone of the company's success was an invention defined by its simplicity: the Brownie. In February 1900, Eastman Kodak began selling this $1 cardboard box containing a spool to hold a strip of film, a small lens, and an easy-to-flip shutter switch. Its inexpensive, rugged construction and ease of use made it a far greater innovation than the Kodak team had dreamed. More than 150,000 Americans snapped up Brownies in the first year of sales. Parents reported: "This camera is so cheap and easy, we can give it to the children!" Plus, the Brownie was perfect for anyone setting out on a trip. When the U.S. entered World War I in 1917, thousands of Brownies traveled to Europe and brought home images of an ever-enlarging world.

In fact, scholars now tell us, their photography was tapping into the basic question of our place in the world—and our connections with others. They were changing self images, one customer at a time, and collectively they were changing global culture. It took the Kodak senior leadership team many decades to grasp that idea. In the post-World War II world, Kodak finally began marketing its core purpose. They asked customers to ask a very basic question: How do you know that an experience with your family and friends really matters? The answer: You want to snap a photo. They both blessed and branded that universal impulse as "a Kodak moment."

So, how did such a model of agile corporate leadership wind up fatally stuck? Kodak actually invented the first digital sensors for film-free cameras, but executives were snagged by their century-old business model selling ancillary supplies. Worse yet, no one at Kodak dreamed of the tsunami-strength disruption on June 29, 2007, the day the iPhone debuted. Suddenly, that quirky Silicon Valley guru Steve Jobs was back on TV and in all the business magazines. Hadn't that guy crashed and burned back in the 1990s when Apple fired him? Yet, here Jobs was yet again, preaching about how the future belonged to "i" products. The nexus of life in the 21st century belonged to "i," which he defined as "internet, individual, instruct, inform, and inspire." He relentlessly lectured other business leaders: This future for this kind of technology is all about each person envisioning his or her place in the world. That's why smartphones had to include not simply the acceptable low-resolution snapshot functions offered on earlier phones—but real-deal, high-quality cameras.

On the iPhone, memorable photos were so easy to take, even a child could snap great photos.

Kodak executives had no time to ponder the irony. They now were hemorrhaging money, which forced them to sell off patents. Waves of layoffs finally led to the 2012 filing for Chapter 11 bankruptcy protection. Remnants of the brand name and a handful of research projects remain, but the giant that once had a near monopoly on photography has fallen.

First, they stalled like deer in the headlights of disruptions in their core business—and finally they were felled by a blow they never saw coming: a phone.

Why the Circus Failed

Kodak is not alone. Dozens of once unstoppable titans of American business fell around the turn of the millennium.

Richard Warren Sears was a railroad station agent when he began selling watches in the era after the Civil War. His genius was instinctively recognizing that there was a valuable link between time, consumer products, and transportation. The first Sears catalog was published in 1888, inviting every American home to connect rapidly with what would become the world's biggest department store. Richard Warren Sears had envisioned the concept that, with 21st-century technology, is Amazon. Suddenly in the late 1800s, the remotest farmer in the Great Plains could shop from home. Then, like Kodak, the founder's vision barely survived the 20th century. One hundred years after its founding, Sears was surpassed by Walmart as America's largest retailer—then Amazon. Today, like Kodak, only a shadow of the Sears giant remains.

The same story now is told about the rise and collapse of American newspapers. That arc stretches back to the rise of the penny press before the Civil War. By the final decades of the 20th century, newspaper chains still were building multi-million-dollar printing plants.

They were unaware that they already had been mortally wounded as an industry. In short, newspaper executives failed to recognize that their core business lay not in printing presses but in the rapid distribution of news and information directly to readers—by any means possible. Newspaper pioneers were visionaries. They joined together to form the Associated Press, among other global networks. There was plenty of time for these titans of data to leverage the internet for their advantage. In 1999, years after the internet had swept into homes nationwide, Google had only a few dozen employees working in their headquarters—a little house in Mountain View, California. The Bureau of Labor Statistics says newspapers collectively employed more than 400,000 people that year. Google was not inevitable; newspapers were stuck and let those agile software developers in an obscure house consume their core business.

The litany of case studies goes on and on.

- Why did Ringling Bros. and Barnum & Bailey Circus close in 2017 after 134 years, while Cirque du Soleil has become the world's largest theatrical producer?

- Why didn't Encyclopedia Britannica become Wikipedia?

- Why did Borders Group bookstores last only 40 years, then crash, in the midst of an era when Americans are buying more print books than ever?

- Why didn't the original McDonald's brothers successfully expand on their brilliant ideas, instead of letting Ray Kroc turn their innovations into a global empire?

- Why did Atari, the inventors of the original mega-hit video game Pong, turn into a nostalgic also-ran in the multi-billion-dollar gaming industry?

- Why didn't Blockbuster snap up Netflix, back when Blockbuster could have swallowed up that little streaming service for pennies on the dollar of Netflix's eventual global worth?

- Why did it take Apple, the top music vendor in the U.S. when Spotify debuted in 2008, until 2019 to surpass Spotify in paying users?

The scope of each story is epic, and they have a common denominator. They needed to move from their core to new stuff but either didn't recognize it or didn't have the knowledge and experience (aka wisdom) to change before it was too late. Can you imagine the evolution of Blockbuster if they had figured out streaming video on demand? Or, at least, if they had had the wisdom earlier on to see Netflix's subscription model as true competition, rather than focus on Apple and Walmart, who were undercutting them on rental and wholesale prices? I don't want to oversimplify the situation and declare Blockbuster would certainly have succeeded but for a little additional wisdom, but read their entry on Wikipedia sometime. It's cringeworthy to see the history of misplaced bets.

When you dive into any of these examples, it gets messy. But that's just business. Even the biggest and best performing firms have their struggles. Remember those jagged lines from the beginning of the chapter? Here's what they look like laid over a chart of the Global 500's profits over the last 10 years.

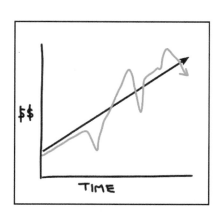

They mostly hug the line, but there are some sharp dips in there. It takes a lot of time to get out of those troughs, to get unstuck. And what doesn't show up here is all of the people and companies and jobs that went away in those low periods because they didn't get unstuck fast enough. But I'm not telling you all this to scare you. The point is, it's very easy to look back after the fact and point out what these and other companies could have done differently.

Let's Be Brutally Honest

I can do the same with my Assurant story. For most of the company's history, we were super successful staying close to our core business, acquiring close competitors, and making steady moves into adjacencies. In hindsight, offering extended service contracts for consumer home goods seems like no big deal; we took what we were best at and applied it in a slightly different context.

But the rapid digitalization of consumer devices hit us like a shockwave. Why? One of the interesting problems we faced was that, although Assurant was one of the world's largest companies in this space, almost no one knew our name. We were a business-to-business service (B2B) in our division. The end users of our policies knew the names of the stores where they had shopped, but our name only appeared somewhere in the mice type at the end of a long agreement most regular people would never even bother to read.

Because no one knew our name, we had no real relationship with consumers. To be brutally honest, that B2B buffer from consumers had let us skate for too long with less than cutting edge service and virtually no digital capabilities. As consumers were quickly learning to expect instant connections via websites, email, text, and live chat—we were still giving customers 800 numbers to call with the predictable queues to wait your turn for an operator. We had multiple operating systems and customer databases, which tended to separate consumer inquiries by product and left their records fragmented in our system. As a result, a consumer could have multiple products with us, phone our help line, and our operator might have no way of finding that consumer's complete profile. From a marketing perspective, this made us ineffective in understanding our consumer's full relationship to the company, so we could not suggest ways they could improve their overall interaction with us. We certainly had no ability to implement more sophisticated marketing opportunities like cross selling products and services.

Those old forms of customer service were beginning to frustrate the very people we wanted to serve: our distribution partners and their end consumers.

It seems so simple in hindsight. I've described our digital challenges in three paragraphs! But when you, like me, are in the middle of being stuck, it can be much more difficult to recognize it. That's why I find all of these examples so powerful and important to share; it's critical that you learn to do something differently and get unstuck before it's too late.

Are You Stuck?

Despite the prevalence of sticking points throughout history, you might be surprised to learn that I get a lot of pushback in those early conversations with leaders when I suggest a company might be stuck. But I don't mind. In the face of that feeling of powerlessness that comes from being stuck, it's hard to open up to some guy who just showed up in your office.

So when I start asking "What are you stuck on?" often the response comes back: "I'm not really stuck. We're moving forward on everything. We just want some help on—" or "We really aren't stuck. We just aren't moving fast enough on—"

This is the time to be intellectually and emotionally honest about where the organization is, the challenges, and most importantly what we *don't* know about how to fix things. Plus, I know that by honestly discussing the core problem of being stuck, we form a bond that builds the trust and confidence we need if we ever hope to march toward future growth.

So I probe the situation in a little more depth. Organizations have developed some powerful defense mechanisms when faced with novel challenges. The more I've discussed this with other executives, the more I've realized these tactics form a vicious circle: the Circle of Stuck.

The Circle Begins

CIRCLE OF STUCK

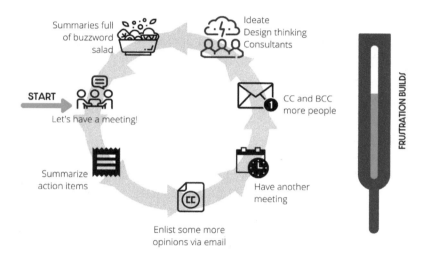

The Circle of Stuck is a vicious cycle, and no matter the company, the industry, the stuck issue, they all typically approach things the same way. It's funny, when I ask people to identify the first thing they do when they get stuck, they all kind of look around, confused. We're not used to thinking of this part of company management as a process. So I usually have to suggest "We have a meeting" and the lightbulbs go off. Of course! I find that stuck companies tend to have lots of meetings, with lots of people, that lead to very little output. Early in the process it seems to make good sense; your company is full of hard working, talented people! Surely if you just put enough brains together...

That's what I thought anyway. At an early point in my digital transformation journey I decided to reach out across our entire staff, sending inquiries to Assurant Solutions offices around the world. Digital was becoming such a huge part of business growth that some of our far-flung employees must know more about this than we did up in the

Atlanta executive suite. I decided we would invest in flying our brightest and best to Atlanta to brainstorm a way forward.

At first glance, this worldwide survey of self-proclaimed experts looked pretty promising. As we combed through our offices around the world, we turned up people who, using their own local initiative, had started to build pieces of the digital puzzle.

I remember one email arrived and I asked a colleague, "Did you know Mexico is building some new websites?"

"Really? Who's doing it?" she asked.

"I don't recognize the names."

My colleague read over my shoulder. "Makes sense: Some of their people just like digital and they're experimenting with it down there. It seems like they have taken it upon themselves to add dial to their "day job." Several are working nights and weekends to build stuff — all outside of their normal responsibilities. How do you want to respond?"

"Send them a couple of tickets," I said. "Let's get them up here. Let's see what they know."

As the responses came back, we saw fledgling projects scattered around the globe. One woman was trying to build a modest digital network over here. A man in another part of the world was studying Internet security. As we dug down into the grassroots of our company, we discovered lots of people were working on this problem. As I read their emails, I could tell these folks were very bright, but I could feel in my gut that they were not united on the bigger existential problem we were facing. There certainly wasn't an overarching digital vision or strategy for the enterprise. Oops. That's my job.

As I reflected on the feedback, the most exciting find was a little startup that our UK division was spinning off under the name Protect Your Bubble. That name caught my eye right away. Whoever the guy was behind that new name—he understood where we needed to push our core business. After all, that's what we sell: protection for the devices you care about in your everyday life.

And so—they came from all corners of the earth. Dozens of men and women gathered in the glass-walled auditorium on the first floor of our Atlanta headquarters. We weren't hiding from the world—or from the rest of our staff. I wanted our other employees to catch the excitement and spread the buzz. I welcomed the questions: Who are those people? What are they saying? What are they planning to do?

Our main goal was to understand a whole lot more about what everyone was trying to do in our offices around the world. We hoped to organize all of that so-far siloed effort into some momentum for the entire company. We had planned the typical agenda for such a gathering: talks, panels and breakouts.

The conversations in those two days at the headquarters felt like rocket fuel. We all knew the stakes. Assurant Solutions had been used to dominating our niches within the insurance industry, but now competitors already were emerging and claiming to be more digitally savvy than we were. So far, it wasn't hard to hit us with that claim. These people I had flown to Atlanta felt the excitement of having been tapped to serve in this telling moment. They had traveled from far and wide for a daring opportunity to change history for our century-old company. Even if we still didn't know how to reach the future—we could at least see our place on the brink of the chasm with a startling clarity.

All eyes kept falling on me. My memory summoned an image of Michael Scott in The Office. There's this episode when the company is headed toward bankruptcy and he gets up at an angry shareholder meeting and starts making wild promises. As the crowd begins to cheer, the promises get more dramatic; he's clearly caught up in the moment. You get the picture! Maybe it was my inner Michael Scott surfacing on that final day of the gathering, but I was intoxicated with the rocket fuel at that point. I wanted to etch our new resolve into the ground floor of that big global headquarters right there in Atlanta.

As I stood to speak, I got this whacky idea to tell them all: "We are going to do this! We are going to be the leader in providing digitally savvy solutions to the markets we serve, and our distribution partners."

I meant what I was saying, right down to my bones. But, I didn't stop there. I kept going. "In five years, 50 percent of our net operating income will come from a direct digital relationship with consumers." It simply felt like this incredibly gifted, hardworking and dedicated group of people deserved an aspirational goal.

I could see the shock on every face. We all knew that, at that precise moment, the portion of our income coming from digital relationships was—exactly zero.

What's more? This was the last day and our gathering, so far, had produced no tangible plan for a digital future.

Then, I saw signs of rising excitement. They caught my vision. My first thought was pure relief. I told myself: Wow! Everybody bought into the idea.

Had I done the right thing? Yes, I had made a fateful decision—but my heart began to race as soon as I was riding the elevator back up to the seventh floor.

Like most CEOs who dare to make such bold announcements and create truly aspirational goals, I closed the door to my office and I just wanted to curl up in a fetal position and suck my thumb. I really had no concrete idea how we were going to accomplish what I had just promised.

News flash: I have shared this story with hundred of leaders in the past few years. Everyone that has been in this place gets it. As leaders, there are times — inflection points— where we need to lay it all on the line to inspire people. It's ok if we don't have it all "figured out."

How Many Emails Do You Send?

Not all organizations have meetings on a global scale, but many have sessions with just as little tangible output. What do we tend to do next? Loop in more people! Have more meetings. Generate lots of emails. And certainly "cc" everyone we can think of.

To demonstrate this point, one executive actually turned her laptop toward me so I could see her email inbox. Her leadership team was cc-ing memos to more than 100 people.

I couldn't help myself. I blurted out, "That's absolutely nuts!"

"Tell me about it," she said with a sigh.

Does this sound like your organization? How often have you settled into your chair in the morning and spent the first two hours sorting and responding to a swamp of emails? As a leader, those two hours represent the most productive segment of your work day. Instead, you've just spun your wheels. And tomorrow morning? Do you even want to think about the inbox you'll open?

Inevitably, someone will move the email thread offline for another ideation session. In one case, I was working with the senior leadership team of a company that needed to morph their product line beyond an overcrowded niche of the market. I was floored when the team described all the work they had done, so far. Somehow, they had stacked up 50 initiatives they claimed to be pursuing—50! And a lot of those had 8-to-10-part strategies. This is actually a fairly common "trick" senior leaders learn. We may think we are winnowing down our options into a concise list by identifying our Top 10 priorities. Then, we add five sub-priorities to each—and right away we have stacked up a mind-boggling 50 initiatives ahead of us.

Again, I was so blunt that it scared them for a moment. I said, "How can you possibly focus on, let alone execute, 50 priorities?"

"Never confuse motion with action."
Benjamin Franklin

Ben Franklin nailed it in those five words. The point is that all that motion we generate through meetings, memos, and action items becomes a proxy for progress—so we can fool ourselves into believing we aren't stuck.

After a moment of stunned silence with that 50-initiative group, I looked around the room and asked, "How did you generate 50 initiatives? Tell me how you got to this point."

The answer was: "Well, over the last few years, we've been working overtime on this problem. We really dug deep. We got a lot of input from everyone on staff and our board weighed in on this repeatedly. We've brought in consultants. We just kept adding the good ideas to the top of our idea funnel. We thought having all those good ideas at the top of the funnel would produce the best outcome."

No one laughed. This was too serious. It was obvious to everyone in that moment of clarity: All their funnel had produced was a clog.

There was an uncomfortable silence. "It didn't work," one of the executives finally said. "And, to be honest, no one is even working on most of those 50 initiatives. Right?"

He looked at each face around the circle. They were nodding at this admission.

Now, let me make this clear: These aren't bad people. We work with incredibly smart folks in major corporations who are trying to tackle some of the most difficult problems in the world. Giants—companies everyone thought were too big to fail—have drowned in these hurricanes.

But it sometimes becomes impossible to break an endless cycle of brainstorming, research, and planning internally. An entire industry has sprung up to compound this kind of activity, under labels like "ideation" or "think tank" or "design thinking." It's no wonder that I often find misalignment in the senior leadership team, and sometimes across an entire company. That's what produces the endless email chains and impossibly long lists of initiatives—stuff that looks like an impressive body of work and gives an illusion of alignment. To be clear, ideation and design thinking are both effective tools. However, leaders often get confused that they are destinations versus tools to help get to the destination.

Buzzword Salad

If a company develops this kind of endless list of initiatives, leaders often wind up turning to external consultants to help gather data on these possible goals. Then, the consultants come back after a lot of time and money with thick decks of information. These investments lead to an extension of the ideation stage. Gathering to talk about the big picture is fun. It's a break from the typical day-to-day, it usually represents a substantial investment by the company, and it makes people feel creative and important. Many consulting engagements wrap with a huge list of potential opportunities for new technology, new markets, new products, new adjacencies, new structures, and all the right buzzwords.

I sometimes wave a red flag when I feel like a leader is just making a buzzword salad: big data, blockchain, AI, internet of things, cloud computing, "_____ as a service," platform modernization, lean enterprise, Industry 4.0. Managers know the shorthand, the cutting-edge initials to toss around in meetings. Their colleagues and subordinates may not be brave enough to admit they barely understand the concepts. The result is lots of big ideas with no implementation plan. That leads to a huge list of new questions: Where should we start? Which team? What return should we expect? And how do we begin?

Everyone feels good as they kick around zillions of ideas—and no one seems to notice we're not moving the ball down the playing field. We're still in the Circle of Stuck.

This leads to frustration. Nowadays, as CEO tenure gets shorter and shorter, emotions can quickly start to flare behind closed doors. People get mad at each other, point fingers and the whole thing spirals to the point of no return.

When I first tell this story to a leadership team, I always see heads nodding in response. One woman looked around at the ceiling of her board room, as if I might have installed cameras. She laughed in exasperation and asked, "Have you been watching us?"

I said, "No. Everyone in your position is facing this kind of problem. The pace of technological change and the real threat of disruption fuel a relentless pursuit of growth—a need to demonstrate momentum to your board, your shareholders, and your entire organization. But even seasoned CEOs with talented senior leadership teams like yours get stuck from time to time. So how do we recognize that your senior leadership team is running in circles? And, what can we do about it?"

To break the circle of stuck you have to acknowledge that the further your company is reaching outside of its core capabilities, the more you have to be willing to change the way you've always operated.

Break the Wheel

What did Assurant look like when we were stuck? A study was conducted and written at the invitation of The Conference Board, the century-old forum for business leaders in New York analyzing our work to bridge the digital divide. The authors were Mary Young and Carey Bongard, Assurant's former head of Global Talent Management and Development. Carey presented it at The Conference Board in 2018. In the words of the report:

> *For a 120-plus-year-old company in an industry where risk management is bred deep in the bone, this was no small undertaking. What would it take to open the minds of executives to the new digital world order? How could the company leap-frog ahead of its competitors?*
>
> *Assurant needed to shift its mindset from being a traditional, paper-based, faxing-and-emailing company to one that met its B2B customers and consumers where they already lived: in the digital world. To get there, Assurant had to shed some of its ways of thinking and working. To protect the company and customers, leaders' knee-jerk response was to poke holes in new ideas. Like many legacy companies, Assurant also placed a premium on getting things right the first time—a value that flies in the face of agile methods. Leaders needed to become more comfortable with uncertainty. At all levels of the organization, people needed to experiment without fear, fail fast, and learn.*

I have come to realize that the intense level of "stuckness" I felt at Assurant was directly related to the enormity of the leap we were looking to make. A top to bottom survey of the company had turned up a lot of passionate people, but we didn't have a concrete vision for what a digital Assurant would look like. When I talk to leaders now about breaking through this Circle of Stuck, I return to some simple sketches on a pad or a white board.

Your core business, core capabilities, are the cozy parts of your operation. These are the set of functions, processes, and capabilities that produce most of the value created by your firm. Over time, you've doubled down, gotten really good at, and have a wealth of knowledge and experience around your core. It has also typically produced at least satisfactory returns for stakeholders.

New stuff—there are lots of fancy consulting terms for this, but I just prefer new stuff—is anything outside of that bubble. It could be pretty closely related to your current business, it could be a new adjacency, or it could be a pretty transformational change. All that really matters is whether you have the knowledge and experience to pursue it. When you don't, you get stuck! And the more knowledge and experience you need, the more stuck you likely feel.

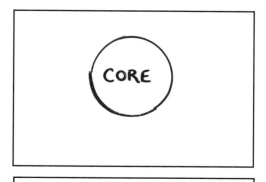

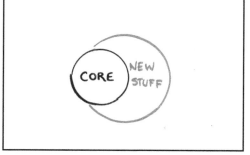

This is the point when the executive points at the charts we've sketched and says, "Wow. Yeah. We really are stuck. In fact, we're stuck on three or four things." It feels like wiping a foggy window with a clean cloth. We've broken through the flurry of activity and acknowledged that something is missing. Something that we need to pursue change efficiently and with confidence.

Pop Quiz

Before I tell you what the magical missing ingredient is, it's time for a pop quiz.

ARE YOU STUCK?

- Yes
- No

You don't get to keep reading unless you check "Yes." That's because the magical part of this secret ingredient is your willingness to admit that you need help. If you can, you're ready to get unstuck!

The Missing Link

There are probably as many definitions of leadership as there are leadership books, courses, and coaches, but when you boil it all down I believe leaders primarily get paid for one thing: making choices. It's the hardest part of the job and something we sometimes look to avoid when circumstances get really uncomfortable. Not that the long list of leadership responsibilities aren't important, but I believe the ability to make timely and successful choices defines the quality of our leadership.

I like the word "choices" versus decisions because it implies opportunity cost. It's not simply picking one of many fine potential paths—your team does that. When they come to you, it's more a binary choice and it involves significant risk. The challenge of leadership is balancing that awesome responsibility with the need to make choices virtually every day. And herein lies our challenge. The speed at which leaders must make choices is ever increasing. On top of that, the complexity of the choices seems to go up exponentially.

So what slows us down? Two things are typically working against us: The further away we move from our core, the more our confidence drops. High confidence tends to mean faster, better choices. As confidence drops, so does our speed. Why? Our personal knowledge and experience becomes less and less relevant as we move further and further from our core. When you're stuck, your knowledge and experience are no longer sufficient to guide you in making confident choices. You slow down. You're missing some much needed wisdom.

It's All About Wisdom

Wisdom may sound like a mystical concept drawn from the ancient past. In fact, wisdom is a timely and pragmatic scale on which to assess both a leader's potential and the need for assistance when the organization gets stuck. Google "the definition of wisdom" and you will find: "the quality of having experience, knowledge, and good judgment." We boil down the ingredients of wisdom into a simple equation: $W = K \times E$.

With this formula, we have reached the turning point in this book. I can sum up our core message, so far, in a single paragraph:

You will probably get stuck, but wisdom can get you unstuck. To be an extraordinary leader, you need a great deal of wisdom. I believe our definition of wisdom is extremely important in the business context. It is the unique intersection of knowledge and experience, not one or the other, not small doses. Large doses of both! Sometimes the extra sources of knowledge and experience you need to increase your wisdom simply do not exist in your senior leadership team—or in the research you have conducted, or the consultants you have hired so far, or on your board of directors, or from your education, your continuing education, or from your networking groups. If you are humble enough to admit you are still stuck, then you're ready to accept help from the wisdom that exists outside of where you'd typically look for it.

Traditional Paths to Unstuck

If you're with me this far, then you've probably bought into my assertion that the wisdom inside your company is sometimes not enough to get you unstuck. Particularly if you are moving away from your core. Instead, the conventional corporate planning process just feeds the Circle. We have more meetings as a leadership team. We get into a room, do lots of brainstorming, and actually sort of beat each other up—everyone tries to sell a solution that someone else should lead. This process tends to repeat itself over and over again—that's why we call it the Circle of Stuck!

The problem is that their knowledge and experience are limited to the core business of the company. Most companies understand this already, which is why they tend to pair strategizing with some internal research and development capabilities. Then they send their people out to learn new things—typically at conferences and networking events.

Back in the heyday of networking, Assurant also invested in networking events for senior-level executives. I enrolled in one of the most exclusive seminar series designed to facilitate peer-to-peer networking. We would show up in a city, listen to a speaker, then spend some time with Q&A. Each seminar then closed with a reception in which the audience—all top-tier executives—were told to go drink and network.

That doesn't sound like a bad idea, but months passed, and I never heard much that was relevant to my work from the podium. So, the speakers weren't much of a draw for me. Naturally, the questions from the floor were largely irrelevant as well. Then, we all were ushered into the reception room, handed drinks and told to do this thing called "networking." What exactly was that? The sound of these receptions was always a loud buzz, punctuated by clinking glasses, but I cannot recall a single worthwhile conversation I had in those rooms. The interactions I experienced were awkward and aimless. Looking across those crowds, how was I supposed to guess which two or three men or women had knowledge and/or experience that could help me? The tendency was for a few extroverts to form circles, monopolize people and head off on tangents that sometimes were entertaining but had no real-world value. The reality is many leaders have the same personality or social style as me: introvert! Yes, we have very public, out-in-front jobs. I certainly loved my role at Assurant. I actually love public speaking and all aspects of being "out front." BUT. At the core, I am an introvert. I would suggest most leaders are as well. The idea of putting me in a large room of strangers with the task of making relevant connections and establishing enough of a relationship for meaningful follow-up is actually ridiculous! When my membership in that seminar series ended, I did not even consider renewing for another year.

So yes, there are probably smart people at these conferences and events, but are you going to find them? To help you with a specific problem? It didn't work for me and I have heard loud and clear from senior leadership teams that they have lost faith in the networking events, summits, and roundtables that were such a fad some years ago. Want to see evidence of that? Google's Ngram Viewer is a handy research tool anyone can use to track the popularity of a word or phrase—measuring the buzz around these terms based on Google's vast database of books, magazines, and websites. The Ngram chart of the "networking" buzz is as crisp and jagged as an Alpine peak. The idea erupted in the 1980s and rose to a huge crescendo in the late 1990s. Since its peak in 2002, however, the popularity of networking looks like a downhill ski run.

This usually brings a stuck company to look even further outside, to consultants. Traditional consulting is a great tool for helping expand the company's base of knowledge. A company may need to know a whole lot more about digital transformation, or new technology, or new challenges in agriculture and nutrition, or about a new market or geography they're hoping to enter somewhere else in the world. The big consulting firms can't be beat on the quantity, quality, and presentation of information on any topic their clients need.

I engaged consultants for my digital transformation challenge. After all, I had just announced to my team that we were going to morph into a digitally savvy company. Do you know what I got back from the consultants? Hundreds of pages on why Assurant needed to become a great digital company. I knew why! I wanted to know *how*. I needed help making choices, not generic models of what other companies were doing.

In a less disruptive business environment, where companies could stay closer to their core business and just focus on efficiencies, acquiring close competitors, or slowly grow into adjacencies, these conventional paths to getting unstuck worked. That's why we have these massive, powerhouse brands in the consulting, conference, and networking group spaces.

But it's my belief that companies have to reach further outside their cores than ever before in order to find meaningful growth. And I further believe, because I've seen it and experienced it myself, that the wisdom we need to do that exists in other people. And often, in places we would never think to look—companies, roles, and people we may have never heard of before.

Hands-on Operators

The difference in my approach to wisdom is to look for it, not in experts, but in operators. What is an operator? The definition is more challenging to pin down than the definition of wisdom. A Google search defines "operator" as: "a person who runs equipment or a machine, e.g., a radio operator." That's not too helpful for our purposes. Wikipedia bounces back a bewildering list of more than 40 possible meanings for the term! The word has been used to describe everything from a role in telephone networks and concepts in mathematics and DNA research— to a Jim Croce hit song and a British indie rock band whose first album was called "What You See Is What I Sell." Merriam-Webster even says the term can be used to describe a "mountebank or fraud." Online searches shed far more smoke than light on the term.

I have actually stopped trying to define them and instead focus on what they have done. Operators that help us get unstuck are simply the people who have gone before us and done the very things we are trying to do. They now have that unique combination of knowledge and experience that we need to get unstuck—to conquer the new stuff we are focused on outside of our core business.

I like to call these narrow streams of wisdom "swim lanes." Envision putting together the pieces of a jigsaw puzzle, matching tabs with gaps. The key is matching the gaps in your existing wisdom with the contours of these operators' years of accumulated wisdom. Melding your wisdom with their wisdom—you generate the power to illuminate pathways to success. Here are some helpful ways my team members have described operators:

"As a group, they are different than scholars or academics. Operators are men and women who have actually worked in the field—who have skin in the game."

"These aren't just experts, because that term often describes people whose role is limited to studying a subject. Operators have studied, but they also have learned by doing."

"These aren't consultants who are trying to chart the future. Operators dared to step into the future ahead of us."

"They're not just smart. Operators possess hard-earned wisdom about what really works—and what doesn't." They have made mistakes. They have learned from their mistakes and built successful businesses.

Across all the professional groups that use the term "operator," my definition is closest to way the U.S. military has been using the term since the 1950s. Each branch of U.S. special operations has its own jargon, but all of them use the word operator to refer to a highly trained man or woman working in operational assignments. Their chief identifications differ, including Rangers, Delta Force, SEALS or Pararescue. However, all branches use the term operator to distinguish between someone actually carrying out missions in the field and someone working in a supportive, non-operational role.

When you're stuck, you need to talk to someone who has actually done the work. To get unstuck as quickly as possible, the most valuable conversation partners are operators.

Solving the Wisdom Deficit

I want to take a moment to acknowledge that the concept of wisdom can feel … dusty. It's long been an idea relegated to the philosophical and spiritual realms. And in truth, that's where my original inspiration comes from.

The Old Testament King of Israel, Solomon, is one of history's most archetypical embodiments of wisdom. When Solomon prayed for wisdom in 1 Kings 3:7-9, he says, "But I am only a little child and do not know how to carry out my duties … So give your servant a discerning heart to govern your people and to distinguish between right and wrong." He chose wisdom over wealth, long life, or honor. Solomon acknowledges right there in verse 9 that it's wisdom that will give him the ability to govern his people, which is demonstrated throughout his story.

Later in chapter 10 of 1 Kings, the bible describes the story of the Queen of Sheba crossing colossal distances (Sheba is modern day Ethiopia!) to meet with Solomon in Jerusalem and see his wisdom first-hand. She showers him with gifts when he answers all her questions, which is one of history's first accounts of a true wisdom-based operator getting someone unstuck!

Another one of the core definitions of wisdom goes back to Socrates. In Plato's *The Apology*, Socrates is quoted, saying "The only true wisdom is knowing you know nothing." This is the jumping off point for philosophical debate. Is wisdom epistemic humility, that you are wise only if you believe you are not? Is it epistemic accuracy, having confidence that you know only and exactly what you actually know? It only gets more esoteric from there!

But wisdom as a definable, measurable quality of human beings is also cutting edge. Developmental psychologist Paul Baltes founded the Berlin Wisdom Project at the Max Planck Institute for Human Development in the early 1980s. Baltes and his group defined wisdom as "expertise in the fundamental pragmatics of life." Most interesting from Baltes' work is how his team measured the five criteria for wisdom. Rather than use surveys and self-assessment, Baltes asked research participants to think aloud as they answered a hypothetical life question. When participants were instructed to engage in dialogue with a person of their choice, or even just to reflect on the problem alone before responding to the life dilemma, they improved their wisdom scores by almost one standard deviation! In this way, the modern research on wisdom lines up with the way wisdom has been represented through the ages; wisdom is demonstrable and able to be developed in dialogue between people.

American psychologist Robert Sternberg has brought wisdom even further into a modern, everyday context. His Balance Theory of Wisdom "defines wisdom as the use of one's intelligence, creativity, common sense, and knowledge and as mediated by positive ethical values toward the achievement of a common good ..." This definition requires the use of traditional learning and knowledge gained through experience to balance the multiple interests and environmental consequences of a decision.

Although currently, our societies tend to emphasize analytical intelligence in their assessments of individuals in school, college, and beyond, one could argue that assessments of wisdom would be more valuable. When citizens and leaders fail in the pursuit of their duties, it is more likely to be for lack of wisdom than for lack of analytical intelligence. In particular, failed citizens and leaders are likely to be foolish—to show unrealistic optimism, egocentrism, false omniscience, false omnipotence, false invulnerability, and ethical disengagement in their thinking and decision making. In other words, they fail not for a lack of conventional intelligence, but rather for a lack of wisdom.

I want to call your attention back to the article I cited in Chapter 2, which illustrated my point about the economic expectations leaders face. The title? "We Need to Solve the Wisdom Deficit in Business." That's my mission and that's what I've been doing for the past several years. The thing is, the business world is full of wise people in their own swim lanes. I'm here to show you how to identify that wisdom and apply it in context to help you get unstuck.

So here we are at the "halfway" point. The book so far has been largely about this thing called "stuck" and a little about my journey. We have also introduced the wisdom formula, $W = K \times E$, which I believe is the only way to truly get unstuck, certainly as you move outside of your core. If you buy into the stuck concept so far, if you buy into my wisdom hypothesis, I encourage you to read on. In Part 2, I describe four simple steps using the formula to get unstuck.

If you're not stuck today, or have a better hypothesis, I wish you all the best! However, if you ever do get stuck, I hope someday you will rejoin me for a few more chapters to see how to leverage the wisdom of others to get unstuck.

Part 2: Unstuck

Get Humble

Admitting that you're stuck—admitting you don't know everything—is a humbling experience. In fact, the Socratic definition of wisdom, "knowing that you know nothing" is the foundation of the concept of epistemic humility. And like wisdom, humility has been relegated to philosophers until recently.

For most of the 20th century, university-based scholars who focused on psychology and social interactions ignored humility. They regarded the concept as a hard to measure, vaguely moralistic quality that wasn't suitable to the rigors of peer-reviewed research. However, psychological research on humility has been growing fast enough to spark a literature review in the October 2019 issue of *Current Directions in Psychological Science*. The authors review intellectual and cultural humility, a personality trait characterized by "an ability to accurately acknowledge one's limitations and abilities, and an interpersonal stance that is other-oriented rather than self-focused." So why should you care? Well, the ability to be humble about your lack of knowledge and experience is the number one prerequisite for success with the wisdom formula. I came to this realization anecdotally, after a few years noting where the model worked (or most importantly, where it didn't work), but now a growing body of research backs me up! Humility is an asset shared by the world's most successful leaders.

Business researcher Jim Collins changed the world's appreciation of humility with *Good to Great: Why Some Companies Make the Leap ... and Others Don't.* Based on five years of research into companies that startled competitors with strong, sustainable turnarounds, Collins declared that humility was not just a factor in their success. It was The Factor. He called it the defining quality in Level 5 leadership, which he ranked at the top of a 1-to-5 scale of leadership qualities. Collins admitted that his research team was "shocked" to discover that an underappreciated, rarely studied quality like "humility" could be so important. Dictionaries equated it with "lowliness," "meekness," and "a sense of unworthiness." It also was suspiciously related to ancient religious values, as an antidote to the deadly sin of pride. Anything that smacked of spiritual thinking was anathema in business schools.

Until Collins rewrote the rules, calling someone a "humble leader" seemed to be an oxymoron. Collins himself admitted to readers that they were in for a surprise. "Compared to high-profile leaders with big personalities who make headlines and become celebrities, the good-to-great leaders seem to have come from Mars," he wrote.

As Collins published his book, he held his breath. Would readers scoff at his findings? The verdict was swift and encouraging. The consensus was: Collins had made a groundbreaking discovery. Without any body of research in scholarly journals on which to rely, Collins and his team had groped their way into uncharted territory. Their findings were especially compelling because they had started as skeptics themselves. How could humility actually be a factor in producing sustained success? To make it onto their list of "great" firms, a company had to have made a major turnaround followed by at least 15 years of sustained growth. The Collins team sifted through the data on one "great" company after another, searched through years of company records and conducted hundreds of interviews.

Collins' team did not expect to run across "humility" in these "great" companies—but it began to pop up in their case studies repeatedly. They began looking for this it-factor particularly in C-suites, the offices where men and women had "C" or "Chief" in their titles. Following the evidence, Collins ultimately placed humility at the top of his leadership scale.

"Level 5 leaders channel their ego needs away from themselves and into the larger goal of building a great company," Collins wrote in his best seller. "It's not that Level 5 leaders have no ego or self-interest. Indeed, they are incredibly ambitious—but their ambition is first and foremost for the institution, not themselves."

Google reports that the term "humility" had been declining in popularity from its peak among writers in the mid 1800s, until a sustained upturn that began around the time Collins' book was released. Now, major foundations are funding studies of humility. An ever-growing number of these researchers are reporting in conference panels, popular leadership magazines, and peer-reviewed journals. Even dictionaries are making it seem more relevant. Merriam-Webster's first definition currently is "freedom from pride or arrogance," which makes humility sound like it actually might be a good thing in an executive.

Over the past two years, "humility" has been popping up regularly in the pages of the *Wall Street Journal* and *Harvard Business Review*. A 2018 *WSJ* news analysis was headlined *The Best Bosses Are Humble Bosses: Organizations are making a push to hire and promote workers who lead effectively but don't seek the spotlight.*

In 2019, Hogan Assessment Systems—which produces psychological evaluation tools for more than half of the Fortune 500 companies—began offering its clients a new "humility scale." Hogan was founded in 1987 by the dean of personality testing, psychologist Robert Hogan. For more than 30 years, Hogan's firm never touched the topic of humility. Now, Hogan's website explains to potential corporate customers that this new scale is valuable when looking for the most effective leaders. "Organizations often overlook humble employees for leadership positions in favor of those who are charismatic. Charismatic people are charming and inspirational, but many turn out to be narcissistic, arrogant, and potentially exploitative. In contrast, humble leaders empower followers and promote team learning."

One of the scholars leading this new appraisal of humility is Peter Hill, professor of psychology at Biola University in California. His work is now widely cited by other scholars.

In 2019, Hill summarized his work so far on his university website. He concluded that the scientific evidence appearing since 2000 defines humility "as a psychological construct that should minimally include three things."

First, the willingness to see oneself accurately, which includes the identification of both limits but also strengths.

Second, an other-oriented rather than self-focused interpersonal stance that appreciates others' strengths and contributions.

Third, a non-defensive willingness to learn from others.

These are peer-reviewed findings backing up what Jim Collins stumbled across two decades ago.

"In study after study, researchers also are discovering evidence lifting up the benefits of humility, while tearing down long-held stereotypes that can have dangerous consequences for the well-being of individuals and nations," Hill wrote in a publicly released report on this research for the Templeton-funded Association of Religion Data Archives. Among the benefits studies are now associating with humility, he listed: "More joy, less anxiety; better relationships; higher self-worth; more effective leaders; and less prejudice, greater tolerance."

We know that humility is an asset for individuals. The research above shows that one of the strongest correlates of individual success is asking how one can get better, can improve. Most people simply don't do it because it's hard.

But this quality can have a much larger, positive impact. So, we are not only talking about humility from an individual perspective, but from an organizational perspective. We know that humility unlocks fresh confidence and creative energy. So, as we approach a new company, we look for humility across the entire leadership team.

How do we judge the level of humility? If you are listening for it, you can tell a lot about whether there is any humility in the corporate culture by how these people talk in a quarterly call or at a trade conference. Are we hearing a silver-tongued presenter who insists that the company has all the answers, the best products—and nobody can touch them? If so, that's organizational arrogance and, if that company gets stuck, then it's not going to look for help in getting unstuck.

So I have boiled down a one-question assessment of a leader's humility: "Can you recognize and acknowledge that you're stuck?"

That's it. That's our humility assessment. Why is that question so vital? If a leader is not willing to admit such gaps exist—or is not open to receiving wisdom from others—then the process won't work.

I can pinpoint the moment I saw humility in action in my team at Assurant as we were stuck on digital. In a way, I made up my own humility assessment before I knew all this stuff.

My team and I were deep in the Circle of Stuck. One day, I'd had enough of gathering in that big meeting room and beating on each other over the latest round of interesting, but ultimately not effective ideas. We were spending so many hours and burning up so much email traffic on this that we were exhausting ourselves without getting any closer to decisions that could bridge the gap. Looking for clarity, I spontaneously did something that is now a core exercise in my work. I asked my team to grade themselves.

I put it bluntly: "Time for honesty. Let's go around the room with an absolutely truthful self-assessment of where we are on this journey. Let's each give ourselves an individual ranking from K to 12 about how much we know about this whole digital world."

There were a lot of anxious faces around the table that morning, so I went first. On a scale of K to 12, my digital expertise was maybe at four—not even at a middle school level. I was inspired by the honesty as others admitted to a lack of understanding.

When everyone had answered, I exhaled a long breath. As a group, we weren't even in middle school in finding this key to our future. As simple as it was, the little exercise made us all fully aware of how seriously we were stuck. Without the right knowledge and experience in the room, our likelihood of success in crafting a digital future was low.

I can tell you from my own experience that there is an incredible freedom that comes from admitting that you don't know everything. If we admit that we don't have all the wisdom ourselves, or in our leadership team, then the question becomes: How can I get more wisdom faster? That's when the real work can begin.

Step One: Get Humble!

Tips

- Put aside ego and know it's OK to not know.
- Learn to be comfortable being uncomfortable.

Exercise

Take a moment to think about a challenge you're currently facing. List the top three things related to this challenge that you don't understand. What, if anything, worries you about admitting you don't understand these things as well as you'd like to?

Draw the Destination

With the prerequisite humility established, we're ready to dive into the practical work of getting unstuck! The process I'm outlining here is almost certainly not the only way to do it, but it has arisen organically from my own experience running Assurant Solutions for 11 years, as well as doing this work over the past few years. I've now seen over 85 flavors of stuck in 12 different industries. And you'll see it's strongly related to my love of using pictures to create clarity.

I'm a visual and interactive learner. As a CEO, I never liked it when someone stood up and lectured endlessly without an opportunity for everyone in the room to engage in the process. That's why I make sure there is a big flip chart or a white board in my meeting rooms. This step is all about discovering, labeling, and sorting your wisdom gaps. People need a clear vision of how these abstract or complex topics—new stuff we're chasing, wisdom we're missing, and operators we could be talking to—connect.

So I encourage you to draw these out yourself as I walk you through it. If you want a little help getting started or just like to keep things neat, you can access printable versions of the charts I describe at the end of the chapter.

Pen in hand, think about the new stuff you're chasing. You've already seen the basic core —> new stuff drawing in Chapter 3, but depending on your company, "new stuff" can be pretty close at hand or way out in outer space somewhere. If we're talking about a whole enterprise transformation, there's probably several points on a continuum of new stuff stretching further and further away from the core business.

Here's a small circle. Let's call that A, your core business. This is where you stand today—what you're good at with all of your assets and liabilities, your strengths and weaknesses. A is what you're organizationally known for right now.

A

What words should we use to label this core? Let's focus on your knowledge, your experience—your wisdom. What do you excel at?

Next, draw a slightly larger circle around the first one. Now we're just outside the core and entering territory where you likely have some goals, some "Point B's." We're looking at products and processes and plans that still are pretty close to your core—but a little reach is involved. There's absolutely no shame in feeling stuck here. The good news is that you probably need the least amount of external wisdom to make significant progress, since your internal knowledge and experience is most directly relevant.

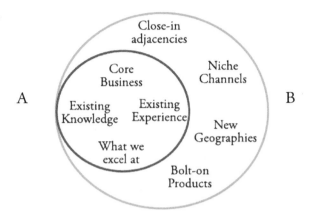

With the third circle we're talking about adjacencies. Maybe M&A ideas you've been kicking around—another company you'd like to merge with or acquire. That could be pretty doable for your team with its current wisdom. Or a new product line that could spring from your core, or a new technology you'd like to bring on board, or a new geography. At Assurant Solutions, we made a conscious, strategic decision to expand globally, including China (more on that later).

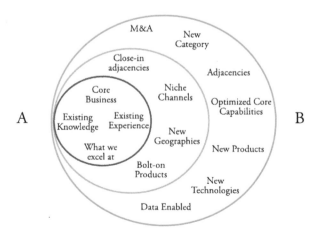

Maybe you can reach most of the stuff in this circle. Maybe.

Finally, a fourth circle. Out here is some stuff that really represents transformational growth. You want to change a foundational part of your corporate culture. Or, enter a new market. Or, tackle a whole new business model. These are all out there on a horizon that's tough for anyone to reach.

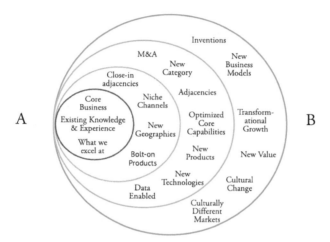

If, like Assurant Solutions, your journey takes you significantly outside of A, your likelihood of getting stuck is pretty big. The reality is that as soon as we venture outside our core, our knowledge and experience go down, and typically not just incrementally, but exponentially. You're trying to reach way beyond your current capacity to change and likely need some help.

You could really call this whole A to B exercise "strategy made simple." Strategy is ultimately more about picking a destination. I don't mean to discount the positive contributions of consulting or design thinking, but anyone can do strategy work. It's the easy part. Not doing it forever is the key. Many companies spend months, quarters, even years trying to figure out what this "point B" should be while the business continues to decline. That's not to say they aren't working hard, but as we've seen from the earlier examples, all of this time spent creating options, ideas, and strategies doesn't get us anywhere. One or more in the pile are probably valid, so pick one! I call this the Strategy Trap. Again; pick one. They are all probably workable and you have to start somewhere. It's critical as a leader to clearly define the destination for your team so that you can start working through what additional wisdom you may need to get there.

Because if you recognize that the likelihood of being stuck is directly related to the distance you hope to reach, you may have caught on to the fact that this is a cycle. When your core capabilities reset, your goals change, and you'll need new wisdom to move the needle again.

If your doodles are anything like mine, you might have a mess of scribbles and still be wondering how this will help you get unstuck. Preferably sooner than later, and with the practical steps laid out in between. Often, it requires not just one person or one answer. Reaching B can take four or five different buckets of knowledge and experience— real wisdom that's not currently present in the room with us—before the team understands all the steps to move from A to B.

So we've basically named the ocean of knowledge we're splashing around in, but I told you to find wise people in their swim lanes. We have to get narrow about what we need to learn.

This part of the process quite literally changed my professional life.

Today, business schools, journalists, and historians point back to 2007 as a milestone in transformative change. That year was as crucial as 1439, when Johannes Gutenberg became the first person in the world to use moveable type. Then, 78 years passed before the impact of Gutenberg's innovation ultimately prompted a German monk, Martin Luther, to ignite a religious, cultural, and political revolution in 1517. In that era, when most people did not live much beyond the age of 30, that meant two lifetimes had passed before the impact of Gutenberg's disruptive technology set off the earthquake of the Reformation.

Compare that with the split-second cracks that shot in all directions from the innovations around the dawn of the iPhone. Thomas Friedman titles a chapter in his new book: "What the hell happened in 2007?" On January 9, that year, Steve Jobs walked onto a stage in San Francisco and declared that Apple had reinvented the phone. While many critics charged that was just Steve Jobs' hype—his announcement actually underestimated the impact of the iPhone. In one direction, that new device began cutting the last remaining legs out from under a tottering Kodak. In another direction, Jobs had suddenly put the vast reaches of the internet into everyone's palm. Other cultural cracks began to form as well. Friedman's chronicle of change in 2007 is breathtaking—even to those of us who lived through it. As that year dawned, Facebook was just beginning to expand beyond campuses and a crazy little micro-blogging platform debuted, even though you couldn't write very much in its tiny screen. Surely it was just a momentary fad! They called it Twitter and lots of smart people thought it was doomed to failure. In 2007, Google itself was flexing its muscles after having just bought YouTube in late 2006—and it launched Android as an alternative to Apple's phone system. Bitcoin was in its infancy that year and, oh yes, before 2007 ended, Amazon dropped the Kindle bomb. Suddenly, Amazon threatened to knock down bookstores nationwide. The vast Borders bookstore chain only lasted a few more years.

As CEO, I needed our thousands of employees to understand just how essential these powerful little devices had become in the lives of millions of people. At that point, I was trying to turn the huge ship of Assurant Solutions in mid-ocean so that we could morph beyond our original nice in credit insurance and extended service contracts to a digitally-enabled business. I had to convince everyone who worked with us that our daily labor ultimately was far more important than just writing insurance policies, paying claims, and all the actuarial and financial stuff that goes along with those efforts. Obviously, that had been our core competency and we were very good at it. But I wanted our employees to realize that our larger market was protecting what matters most—and that was quickly becoming their smartphones.

Then, in what seemed to be a weird change in our culture, those new smartphones suddenly soared to the top of the list of what people felt they needed to survive. People began telling researchers that their smartphones ranked as the top one or two most important things among the necessities they owned. Depending on your perspective, that data was either a sad comment on our culture—or it was an opportunity unlike anything we had seen before that time. If your dryer broke down, you might wait a while until you could afford to replace it. But your phone? If that died, you wanted to replace that same day.

I wanted to dramatize this point in my talks.

I will never forget the gasps of horror when I threw that iPhone into a blender and pushed: PUREE.

When I began destroying smartphones in front of our employees, I certainly could not see the future as clearly as Friedman now describes it in his page-turner about the pace of business disruption after 2007. What I did know at the time was: This level of change was going to disrupt the core of our business—and I sensed that a lot of this was going to revolve around our sleek new phones. My instinct was that there was a golden opportunity in all that disruption.

Meanwhile, I've already shown you what was going on behind the scenes. My team and I were stuck. I was gathering all this momentum to go ... where exactly? There were several big steps missing between Assurant Solutions' A and B.

This is when I bumped into GXG and this wisdom-based learning methodology, as we call it today. GXG also introduced me to the concept of a learning ecosystem—simply put, a small group of people (operators) who had wisdom in the specific areas where we were stuck.

Was I immediately convinced this was going to chart our way forward? Honestly, no. But at least it seemed like an approach worth pursuing. (It was. I eventually retired after many years at the helm of Assurant Solutions; then I bought GXG to try to build this new kind of team into an international powerhouse.)

You know already that I'm a visual person, so I believe some kind of physical map is essential when we're talking about abstract concepts. Once you know where you're trying to go, you can begin to analyze the wisdom gaps between your core and that destination. At GXG, we call this a learning ecosystem or a knowledge map, although those phrases are widely used by others and have a variety of meanings. It's really just a style of mind map which we use to display our clients' wisdom gaps. They're a tangible thing we can gather around and confirm that we're aligned to the same learning goals and priorities.

Mind maps help you grasp a big picture overview of the subject under study, reduce mental clutter, help you cope with information overload, and help trigger creative associations between seemingly unrelated bits of information.

In other words, mind maps are a perfect tool to help you get started on your journey to unstuck! If you've never heard of mind mapping before, there are TONS of resources online to explain the concept (and sell you software). But I want to walk you through how a mind map can help you work through complex topics like business strategy or technology implementation.

You also could think of the chart as a reverse treasure map. We place the gold in the center and we work outward as we collectively sketch all the gaps we have to cross to reach that goal. As we identify the first major gaps, we spot other more-specialized areas of expertise we will need, as well. As we sketch all of this, we can see a webwork emerge of the kinds of experts we need to find.

Here's a few guidelines as you build your own ecosystems.

Start with the destination you decide on through the earlier A-B drawing. That's the topic in the center of your paper, the thing you're stuck on, whether that's a technological, operational, or transformational challenge. Enterprise transformations necessarily unify technology, operations, and people/change management strategy—that's a lot to map all in one! Feel free to break it down into smaller, component ecosystems, or else keep your combined picture high level. (No more than three levels deep.) If you do them separately, you may be surprised at how many points you find where they all connect or overlap.

Other examples for maps you might want to create, depending on your destination, include 3D printing, new business integration, or finance function transformation. I recommend you do this on paper or a white board to start. It doesn't have to be pretty! The real benefit is in thinking through the components of your business challenge and how the buckets of wisdom you need are related (or not).

If you've been stuck for any length of time, I bet you've collected quite a bit of information around your challenge. Making a mind map is your opportunity to make that reading work for you! Pull out the ideas from each source that really resonate with you, make connections between them, and discard the rest. The way your industry talks about the topic and what's trending in that topic area at large give important context to the kinds of wisdom you might be missing. Unless you have several major ideas that very clearly branch off from your main topic, try starting with just three or four.

Just like with the Circle of Stuck, it's critical you know when to stop. The biggest temptation as you build out each major branch in detail is to record a node for every scrap of information you read. When you are in your second and third layers of detail, be a strict editor. For example, when I map automation for a client, I almost certainly include AI, machine learning, and RPA as subtopics, because differentiating between these technologies is important. Most client challenges, however, do not call for a distinction between machine learning models like neural or Bayesian networks, so I don't include them. The more you look, the more connections you see. It can be helpful to show how some concepts are shared between branches but draw lines for only the most important ones. It's more useful if your mind map is clear and elegant.

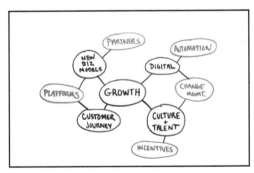

Assuming you want to use this mind map as a way to communicate with team members, spend a little time making a cleaned-up version. Then build a companion document with links to the resources you referenced in its creation. This enables anyone to see your logic without you having to explain it.

I work regularly now with leaders in Fortune 500 companies and this process really resonates with executives who have experienced other forms of consulting. The focus here is on charting a simpler, clearer, pragmatic process that makes sense as a way to help their team actually go out and achieve results. One way we test whether we're on the right track is a little exercise in probability. Leaders seem more comfortable assessing probability than directly asking for help.

We might ask a question like this: "If we don't find someone to help you with online security, what's the probability you will succeed in that particular area?" People usually respond honestly to that kind of question.

A quick poll of the leadership team might result in odds of 4 out of 10 for succeeding without help. Although the question was indirect, the answer is eye opening. We do this for each of the component parts of the ecosystem and then again for the entire "stuck" topic. The average score after three years doing this exercise is less than 70%, meaning there is a less than 70% chance of getting unstuck without the necessary wisdom on the team. People will spontaneously say things like: "Well, no wonder we're moving at a snail's pace!" But, the purpose of this is not to assess blame. We have already diagnosed that they are stuck—and we also have consensus on the goal, the point B they are trying to reach. So, this question about probability is just a practical way to identify the gaps in reaching B.

After such a quick probability poll, we would say: "So, the team agrees there's only a 40% likelihood you can handle that aspect of the overall project without help. Let's make sure we find someone who's wise about that specific issue." Around the room, some heads will be nodding. As we add that circle to the growing map, we remind the group that we define wisdom as having both knowledge and experience working in the field. "We can find someone good to help with this," we say. More heads are nodding now. We have consensus that this should be a circle in the knowledge map.

The example map above represents gaps often faced in a digital transformation—not unlike what we faced at Assurant Solutions. Our wholesale distribution model was primarily through banks and dealers. That meant we needed to switch from brick-and-mortar to focus on e-commerce, and learn about digital business models and the potential industry impacts, and think through the implications for the company's strategy, culture, and structure.

GXG created a Digital Advisory Board (DAB) for Assurant Solutions, with the goal of designing a strategy for digital distribution, both direct to consumer and e-retailers. After we spent some time establishing a common digital language, or, what going digital would mean specifically for our company, the DAB began to work on the following:

- Transforming the customer experience and engagement strategy
- Data monetization strategies
- Branding and vision
- Recruiting and retaining top digital talent
- Application of automation technologies

The ecosystem visual showed us the interconnectedness of all these topics and also helped guide us to the people who would sit on our board and the voices we would need to add to the conversation as we evolved.

One final note about these ecosystems: When GXG works with clients, our success metrics match theirs. This means we only work with people if we can reasonably expect to help them get unstuck. At its core, then, we have to define the problem in a realistic way. We have to benchmark our expectations across a client's industry, and sometimes across various industries. But, ultimately, these are highly personalized tools. Your map may not make sense to anyone outside your organization! So let go of needing to get it "right." If you are thoughtful about what wisdom you need to succeed, this map will help you find it.

Step Two: Draw the Destination

Tips

- Define the destination. What's your B? How far are you trying to reach beyond your core capabilities?
- Design your personal ecosystem.
- Center your challenge.
- Use your research.
- Add detail, but don't get in the weeds.
- Make it shareable.

Exercise

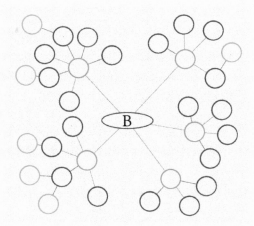

To download printer-friendly PDFs of this exercise, visit: www.craiglemasters.com

Smart People Ask for What They Need

Until now, this process I'm teaching you has been relatively DIY. You don't really need me (or anyone else) to dig deep for some humility, hit pause on the flurry of stuck activity, and define your goals in terms of distance from your core knowledge and experience. A lot of the teams I work with are perfectly able to map their wisdom gaps without GXG's input—the benefit of all that prior brainstorming, research, and consulting.

But here's where I sometimes hit a slowdown. It's time to profile and identify some people—operators—to have candid conversations with about some humbling challenges. It can be really exciting to scour the internet for experts and even more so when you realize there are people swimming in some of the narrow lanes of wisdom that would be hugely beneficial to you on your journey. But when it comes to drafting that outreach note ... maybe you'll just do a little more looking around ... It's really tough to reach out cold and potentially invite a stranger into a sore spot in your professional life. Recent research also is underlining the difficulty in prompting people to take these first steps toward asking for help.

University of Michigan sociologist Wayne Baker has worked inside universities, companies, and nonprofits, training internal teams in techniques to optimize their helpfulness. "I can tell you from all of our research that generosity isn't the problem," Baker says. "We know that most people are willing to help. The real problem is getting people to ask for what they need. People don't know how to make such a request—or they feel uncomfortable asking for help. Why? There are lots of reasons. Often, we don't ask because we fear that people will think we're incompetent if we ask for help. But, that's simply not true. Research shows that—if you ask—you will be perceived as more competent. Smart people ask for what they need."

One of my own passions is pointing out to leaders that they don't know everything—and then reassuring them that's fine, because they're not *expected* to know everything. Knowing everything is not possible—and knowing everything is not the definition of a successful leader. Leaders are defined by the choices they make. Among the most important choices are recognizing the wisdom in others. That's a foundational truth in the work that we do.

That's why mapping the learning ecosystem is so essential. Each circle we draw in this gap analysis sets our team on a quest. To fill that circle, we are looking for the right expert to help us fill a gap that will push us ever closer to our goal.

Let's say your internal research and your consultants are telling you to build a new plant—maybe in an entirely new location where you haven't established a footprint. Before you commit all those millions, wouldn't you want to talk to three or four people who have tried to build plants in that same part of the world? Among those operators, wouldn't you want to talk to a couple who succeeded—and maybe also someone who failed? Don't you want to know what they know before you choose to commit your own resources? And, don't you need to hear from them right away—as rapidly as possible?

We answer those questions. We find the people who have the hard-earned wisdom needed to fill those gaps. When people hear that the crux of what we are doing is tapping into external operators for a carefully managed transfer of wisdom, one response can be: "Well, that sounds wonderful, but it's an idea that almost goes without saying, doesn't it?"

I agree to a point. It is radically simple. But I'm giving away the toolbox to you in this book because I know everyone won't run out and do this tomorrow, transforming business forever. It still takes time, discipline, and honestly a lot of work to draw out the humility in the first place.

Where Are They Swimming?

So where do you find these people? And what do you look for?

Here's another place where some traditional learning resources can work for you. The true key is engaging the people you find there in a different way. So your professional network is a valid place to start, with this caution: everybody believes they have a network—even if that network has never done a thing to help them.

That's why I advise you look for people you would not normally regard as a peers. That may sound like an odd choice. After all, for decades, "peer networking" has been a mantra among management consultants. The flaw in peer networks is one that Gen. George Patton observed repeatedly during World War II: "If everybody's thinking the same way—nobody's thinking." The chances for successful innovation shrink dramatically if you only interact with people you regard as peers.

Years of research have shown that self-defined peer networks increase the likelihood of bias. Consider this question: How many of these problem-solving strategies show up in one form or another in your organization's discussions at the highest levels?

- Intuition
- Rule of thumb
- Educated guess
- Common sense
- Trial and error
- Personal experience
- Consensus of peers

These all are heuristics, common methods for making quick decisions. They may prove useful in many instances—but all of these strategies are infamous for encouraging biases that can fatally flaw your outcomes.

Over many years, scientists have categorized dozens of biases that can creep into decision making through these methods.

Some of them have fancy names, like the Semmelweis reflex. That's a bias named for the Hungarian Dr. Ignaz Semmelweis who discovered in 1847 that infant mortality rates fell dramatically if doctors simply washed their hands in a chlorine solution before procedures with patients in a maternity ward. Some of his peers were offended and refused to follow his advice, because they would not believe that germs could be transmitted by a gentleman's hands. The bias is called a reflex because it's a knee-jerk reaction to anything that assaults our basic assumptions about life.

Some biases sound downright funny, like dogfooding. That's a real-world term for the bias that stems from the business axiom that employees should "eat our own dog food." The value of the original marketing strategy is obvious. If a company's own employees don't like to use their products, there is probably a major problem brewing for the whole company. However, the dogfooding bias creeps in when too many people migrate toward the official product line and the organization loses the ability to appreciate the potential popularity of competitors' brands. Kodak executives could not believe that the world would turn its back on those beloved "Kodak moments." Everyone they knew loved Kodak products and assumed they would forever remain a part of family gatherings. Kodak leaders were dogfooding their strategic decisions, discounting the need to rapidly adapt to a changing global culture.

Some terms for biases have been reduced to initials like NIH, for "not invented here." Many leadership teams slow innovation due to a bias toward developing everything from scratch—reinventing the wheel—even when cutting-edge parts and processes are available from other providers. This bias might manifest as a nationalist bias against foreign companies. It is equally fatal when NIH blind spots prevent leaders from even looking for ready-made resources closer to home from other companies. The most successful software developers today have learned to avoid this bias and leapfrog new products into the market by using components available from other vendors.

Long lists of biases fill entire books on decision-making. If they are properly understood, biases can become crucial insights for marketing efforts. Seth Godin built his concept of "permission marketing" around the challenges of customer bias. At Duke, Dan Ariely explores both the dangers and the possibilities of biases in his lectures and his books about choice architecture.

The key to disarming the dangers of biases is understanding how perniciously they weave themselves into the top levels of our leadership teams. Greg Satell recently wrote about several of the biases that have hamstrung Fortune 500 companies. Chief among them, Satell argued, is availability bias. This stems from a common problem-solving strategy of summoning the best wisdom from the most available data. That sounds like a savvy way to make decisions. It turns into a deadly bias when that data is fundamentally flawed by limitations no one could discern. In one of Satell's case studies, he points to the example of Coca-Cola executives in the 1980s, who were convinced by an extensive series of taste tests that consumers would flock to a new flavor of Coke. What they were missing was data on the nostalgic loyalty of millions of customers to Coke's original taste. No one seemed able to measure that overwhelming preference for classic Coke before the big switch was made. The flavor changeover proved to be a marketing disaster, even though all the available data predicted a huge hit.

Many researchers like Satell point to availability bias as a cornerstone of bad decisions—from the Edsel to the short-lived Google collaboration platform called Wave. Some of the world's smartest people launched those products with confidence based on all the evidence available to them at the time—and realized only later that they had misread the market. All too often, our human sense of the best available data relies too heavily on the people we consult in our inner circle.

So your aim in finding wise people should be to deliberately break down silo walls for these new connections. Use the power of conversation with people outside your organization to break down biases.

All warnings aside, where *should* you look? Wherever there are people who have done it before you. It's rare, in my experience, that a challenge is so unique, and so industry specific, that there is no one in the professional world with insight on it. OK, OK, you likely understand that there is someone, somewhere in the world who can help you, but how do *you* find them? What lakes and ponds are your experts swimming in?

This is another place where some of those traditional resources become helpful again. Look back at the research you've compiled while stuck, and especially while building your ecosystem. Look up the authors. Do a web search around your key initiative, say implementing a cloud platform, and read vendor and corporate press releases. Do they quote any key personnel? Look at conference agendas. Start in your own industry, but also branch out—after the keynotes, conferences have so much time to fill that sessions become deeply specific. You not only get a little peek into the machinery of how other companies operate, you get the names of the people who have the most direct and relevant experience.

One major benefit of this era of the "personal brand" is that the web, and social media like LinkedIn, make it so much easier for people to show off their professional passions. I guarantee there is some public-facing content put out there by someone you'll be excited to talk to. In fact, if you're willing to let go of some of the specifics, you'll even need to narrow down a whole list of people! They key is to ignore that little bit of ego that keeps you hung up on the details of your challenge, in your company, your role, your budget, etc. For example, I have worked with clients in banking who are convinced that this or that regulation is a uniquely frustrating obstacle to how the process, store, or share data. And they are well connected in their industry and everyone else they've talked to feel the same. Well, that's when I ask if they've talked to anyone in healthcare—another tightly regulated industry with similar data challenges.

Once you open up your perspective in this way—as I said, it takes a little extra dose of humility—you can start being picky. After all, you're not simply looking for the most knowledgeable and experienced person you can find. You're looking for someone who will be open to help, and ideally a pleasure to talk to!

Generalized Reciprocity

"OK," I can hear you thinking, "Some professional outside of my industry wants to help me get unstuck? Why would they do that?"

The answer is: They want to help, because people are more generous than we may assume. Today, a growing number of successful veterans in the business world increasingly see the value of helping others. At GXG, we have accumulated years of anecdotal evidence of this trend. With each passing year, we can back that assertion with a growing stack of research.

When one of our team members reaches out to strategically placed men and women in leading corporations around the world to ask if they would be willing to help a stranger in a one-hour telephone call—the answer frequently is: "Yes."

Usually, these people are eager to help, quite simply, because helping is a part of their own core values. How do we know that?

We are relying on what sociologist Dr. Wayne Baker at the University of Michigan's Ross School of Business calls "generalized reciprocity." Others sometimes describe this concept as "paying it forward"—doing something to help others without any immediate expectation of a payback from the person we are helping. Baker says, "Direct reciprocity is when I help you and you help me—and the reciprocity is direct between us. In contrast, generalized reciprocity is you help me, then I feel grateful and help a third person and that person helps a fourth person."

Baker's research of generalized reciprocity in business now is widely cited in prominent journals, business magazines, and books. His findings pop up in business courses nationwide. This led Baker to co-found Give and Take, a company that provides training methods to optimize this effect within existing organizations. Their methods are used in a long list of Fortune 500 companies and leading universities, including the Harvard Business School. In 2019, U of M's Board of Regents invested $500,000 in Give and Take to further expand this work.

In his TED Talk, Baker responds to critics who have argued that there is a more cynical motive driving reciprocity. Instead of sharing in a good feeling of generosity that makes people want to pay it forward—critics have said that people actually are getting paid back right away in a commodity called "reputational incentives." People who help a stranger are doing this mainly to look good to the rest of the world. In other words, Baker's critics say there's a lot of hypocrisy involved in helping others.

In response, Baker says, "We designed a study to be like a horse race, analyzing data on business decisions to see if people were helping others mainly because of reputational incentives or mainly because of a feeling of generosity. We looked at 44,000 decisions and both incentives were found to be a factor in the race—but the gratitude horse crossed the finish line 10 lengths ahead of the reputational horse. Gratitude is a far more powerful force leading people to help each other than reputational incentives."

In addition, Baker's one-time doctoral student Adam Grant is now a professor himself at the Wharton School and has built on his mentor's research. In his best seller, *Give and Take*, Grant busts the old dog-eat-dog business myth. In one study after another, Grant has found that professionals who are "givers" wind up rising to the top in greater numbers than "takers." It's time to dump the old stereotypes, Grant argues. "Although we often stereotype givers as chumps and doormats, they turn out to be surprisingly successful," he writes.

Certainly, a motive for some people is that they want to be regarded as 'thought leaders' by their colleagues. So, being asked to give us a free hour of their time to help someone in another company is a sure sign that they are regarded in that way. It's self-affirming. That's one motive.

But this really works mainly because of a much deeper understanding of the world as a whole network of relationships. I recently got to speak to a group of soon-to-graduate students at Georgia Tech and I was so encouraged by how they want to steer their careers in the direction of valuing and fostering relationships. They want to help people, whether anyone is noticing everything they do or not. This reflects how I see the larger world. The truth is there really are people who want to help.

I got to experience that willingness to help firsthand when we assembled Assurant's first Digital Advisory Board (DAB) members. Now, I also did the kind of one-on-one learning I'm advocating for you and it was an overwhelmingly positive experience. You can read more in the next chapter. All the advisory board program did was put all of the wisdom in one room at the same time.

As a reminder, to get to the B-state for Assurant, we had some significant wisdom gaps. We needed to know how to build an e-commerce component into our business. We needed to develop a common understanding of digital throughout the organization. And I needed my senior leadership team to have more exposure to the implications of digital for our overall strategy, culture, and structure. From our side of things, the DAB would consist of me and my senior leadership team. And here's who GXG invited to share their experience, expertise, and most importantly, their candid evaluation of our strategies, for that first meeting in 2014:

Mobile Marketing Pioneer

Digital Marketing Expert

Global Product Leader

eCommerce Exec

Consumer Trends Designer

Enterprise Data Lead

Hopefully it's clear from their profiles how these people had the wisdom we needed to get unstuck: a mobile marketer, enterprise social media strategist, consumer behaviorist, digital business leader, B2C expert, and an enterprise data analytics executive. I know I was increasingly excited as we assembled this list. Maybe … just maybe, this group of unbiased, wise people could be the secret to getting unstuck!

Step Three: Find the Wisdom ... and be Specific

Tips

- Review your prior research and conference agendas for names of people who are (obviously) passionate and actively involved with your challenge.

- Do web searches with the key words from your ecosystem, your wisdom gaps. If any articles resonate with you, look up their authors.

- Explore people's online presence for signs of:

- curiosity or engagement with their industry and trends.

- a focused career with one technology, role, or expertise (e.g. a digital team leader who emphasizes their recruiting and retention practices).

- Reach out with something specific and relevant you've read about another person's work, to show your genuine respect for their time and attention.

Exercise

What are you an expert in? Is there someone in your network you could offer to help through conversation?

'Thinking Outside the Building'

I'm thrilled that you're still with me, which hopefully means you've bought into the first three steps: embracing humility, defining your destination, and searching for the wisdom that you're missing. But now we're shifting gears to how we actually activate that external wisdom. Now that we have found these very wise people, how do we actually engage with them and, crucially, absorb all of that knowledge and experience? I'm not unaware that what I'm asking you to do is challenging. After all, it's the key part of the process that I get paid for! The ability to mobilize partners across challenging situations and innovate in the face of establishment paralysis is an advanced leadership skill, identified by Rosabeth Moss Kanter in her latest book *Think Outside the Building*. To engage these experts you'll have to be a little bit flexible and creative, open to suggestions that may sound unworkable in your current organization, or even just a little wacky. That's what really makes these conversations spark change.

I've talked about the Digital Advisory Board (DAB) some and the impact that it made, but actually before I engaged the board I did exactly what I'm teaching you to do here. One on one, GXG connected me with a group of executives who had successfully established businesses in China.

All around the world, people were embracing our Assurant Solutions warranty products. We had moved successfully into Latin America, Europe, and other parts of the globe. We knew all about the complex process of moving into new markets. That is, until we launched in China. How did we get stuck there in the first place?

Best Buy, one of Assurant Solutions' clients in Canada, is a great case study of how challenging the Chinese market is. Best Buy could never get traction, analysts say, because of a cultural mismatch between Chinese consumers and Best Buy's own brands, prices, and policies. The growing Chinese middle class definitely had money to spend on their products, but Chinese consumers knew little about Best Buy's approach to merchandizing. When consumers did visit their stores, they often walked away because of the cultural clash. After Best Buy left, one of the executives admitted to the *Wall Street Journal* that the failure was largely due to "arrogance" that Best Buy could re-educate Chinese consumers about their approach to doing business. As I read that *WSJ* story, I thought: There's another reminder of the crucial need for humility in business.

After we launched in China and began looking for new clients, we discovered that forming business relationships in China involved a different set of cultural assumptions. We also struggled with government restrictions. These regulatory standards were especially concerning because Chinese laws governing business are vague by design. We wound up paying a lot of money to lawyers who would give us advice like: "Well, we think the laws sort of say this. But then they also sort of say that. We think your risk is reasonable." That's hardly a reassuring assessment for a CEO trying to decisively expand in a new market. The best we can tell you is: "*Maybe* it's OK?"

That's not good enough. By the way, that was an actual conversation … with a $700 per hour lawyer!

China remained a great prospect. Based on our successful expansions across Latin America and Europe, I assumed we could do quite well in China. We were already making progress in Japan and we were starting to work in South Korea. Annual studies of Chinese consumer spending showed an ever-growing desire for electronics, appliances, cars, and other goods we could protect. The consultants we hired came back with a very persuasive deck of data that concluded: Yes, our business should grow in China. Our leadership team was convinced that an investment in China was important long term. All the data lined up in favor of growth.

We just could not get traction. It was as if we were exploring a galaxy far, far away where even the most basic assumptions about life and work had shifted. My own knowledge and experience in international business wasn't getting us anywhere. My senior leadership team was not familiar with China's rules and cultures. We had consultants on board to help, but we still were stuck.

We already were working with GXG on building our DAB—so the GXG team offered to help with China, as well. They agreed to arrange series of one-hour conversations through their Direct Connections program. These are facilitated conversations with wise people for the sole purpose of sharing their knowledge and experience. Our China conundrum was a great opportunity to test that system. At first, I was skeptical that a series of phone calls would make much of a difference. It turned out that the real value in these calls was the quality of the people on the other end of the phone. I wasn't talking to consultants or leadership coaches anymore. I was able to talk at a very practical level with real-world operators.

The GXG team mapped out a learning ecosystem with me—the same kind of chart you see in Chapter 7—copied for you below! To view a full-size printable version, visit www.craiglemasters.com.

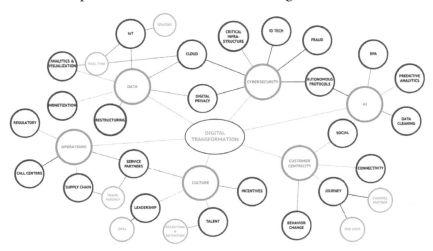

This chart shows one big circle labeled "Digital Transformation." Off that hub, the GXG team's research identified 11 operators around the world who could unlock specific puzzles on which we were stuck. I received detailed bios of these people. Then, one by one, calls were arranged with these operators.

And my initial question was: What can I possibly hope to learn in a one-hour conversation?

What's the ROI on an Hour?

We hear this question all the time—and with good reason. Today's business leaders face an overwhelming wave of meetings and messages every day and are skeptical that they will see a positive return on their investment of the time they spend in any new interactions. Plus, there are a couple well established companies offering on demand expert networks and scrappy new entrants with better platforms, more experts, and faster responses popping up all the time. How could GXG or this process I'm teaching you be any different?

It partially comes down to my emphasis on that word "conversation," which refers to far more than a casual invitation to chat or transactional information dump. Nearly 2,500 years since Socrates perfected his method of teaching through conversations, people are still grappling with the best way to use this timeless method for transferring wisdom. The International Listening Association (ILA)—the global network of scholars who study the essential give-and-take of listening—cites a long list of research that proves the value of listening in any successful life, including in business. The ILA also cites studies revealing the many modern barriers to holding an authentic conversation. Finally, these scholars decry the fact that most U.S. schools don't require students to receive training in active listening.

This is a real problem in business, writes Greg Satell, author of *Mapping Innovation*. "Schools don't teach communication. They teach math not very well, some science, history, and give rote instructions about rigid grammar rules, but give very little guidance on how to express ideas clearly," Satell concludes. That leads directly to senior leadership teams in big businesses discovering that they are stuck in circular communication. Usually, they wind up leaning on dangerous biases. Innovation requires breaking out of those closed loops through meaningful communication with others.

As a culture, we are so focused on the latest technology and the hottest new apps that we wind up raising a tidal wave of information that washes over us each day. We hardly have time for a meaningful talk with another person. Evidence of our collective struggle to reclaim this valuable learning tool is the popularity of "conversation" as a theme in scores of articles at the *Harvard Business Review* (HBR). Why do HBR writers touch on this topic so frequently? Because, as HBR reported in 2019, the global size of the workplace-training industry has grown to more than $360 billion per year. Despite that enormous investment, learning has stalled in many organizations. The consensus among these workplace educators is that business leaders need to expand their capacity to learn. And, those improvements start with—conversations. A recent survey on workplace learning found that workers are 67% more likely to go to their professional network rather than their companies' learning systems to build skills. Our point precisely.

Bain & Company's Michael Mankins laid out the problem in his own recent HBR column about processing the information around us, titled "Is Technology Really Helping Us Get More Done?" His answer, in one word: No.

"As the cost of communication decreases, the number of interactions increases exponentially, as does the time required to process them," Mankins writes. As recently as 1990, an executive might have to deal with 20 messages a day, or 5,000 a year. Today, that number of communications via voicemail, email, texts, and social media may be more like 50,000 a year, Mankins calculates. On top of that 10-fold increase, leaders also are spending more time than ever before attending in-person or digitally connected meetings—many of which are poorly planned and moderated. The result, Mankins writes, is that "bad behaviors or poor procedures for sharing information" are leaving many organizations stalled.

I firmly believe history is on our side here, that this is the way we're supposed to learn! One-on-one or small group discussion formats have been carried forward from ancient times as a way to explore advanced concepts and develop critical thinking. Most famous, per-haps, is the Socratic method, a foundational part of legal education to this day. Socrates' student Plato is actually the first known user of the word "dialogue" (*dialogos*) and founded the first institution of higher learning in the Western world. Modern theories of dialogue education embrace this model's significance of engaging learners, acknowledging them as decision makers, and in setting achievement-based objectives. Conversational learning is uniquely shaped around what the learners will ultimately do with content and learning tasks, or open questions that need to be explored. Most importantly, this is not another stream of data washing over you.

At GXG, we developed our process specifically to relieve the power-less feeling of passive information intake. In the midst of being stuck, with the sheer volume of daily noise generated in searching for a solu-tion, a one-hour facilitated conversation feels refreshing! Especially when it empowers you to sift through more and more of that noise thanks to the practical wisdom exchanged.

What's Your China?

All that noise is why I decided to try something new. Why not give GXG's Direct Connections series a chance? The calls GXG arranged all took place some years ago, but the one call I remember vividly was with a Xerox executive vice president, who then was in charge of his compa-ny's Asian operations.

The result was mind-blowing. This was my real "Aha!" moment. After a few minutes of introductions, he got down to the practical nuts and bolts. I gave him specifics of what we were trying to do. He started giving me names of Chinese regulators we should talk with—and what to avoid in approaching regulators. He checked off a list of potential cultural mishaps, and how we could find our way past those pitfalls. I remember thinking, halfway through the call: I've got a stack of books and consulting reports on my desk all about doing business in Asia and in this brief conversation, I've already got more useful advice than in all that reading! The catalyst was that he had been working in Asia for many years; 25, in fact. He had lived there. I was soaking up every single minute of his advice—and he kept checking off one box after another: ideal locations, tips on hiring people, tips on interviewing people, tips on firing people, on and on. I realized that, top to bottom, so many things we take for granted in other markets are completely different in China.

When we were done, I remembered all of the expensive global seminars I had attended with other CEOs where we were supposed to go figure out our own style of networking over cocktails or some other seminar format. I could not recall getting anything of great value out of those long and expensive sessions. This call with this one executive was game changing for me. In addition to the valuable insights he shared with me in that hour, I now knew he and I could call each other in the future if something else arose. As it turned out, I talked with him several more times. Now, about five years have passed since we last talked, but I know he could reach out to me today—or I could reach out to him again—and both of us would remember our conversations. We would be ready to help each other, once more. Over a six month period, through my 1:1 operator calls I received the wisdom of over 125 years of collective experience in China. That's W = K x E in action!

Please do not underestimate how fast you can learn. The way most of our formal education is structured now, we've been conditioned to believe learning—especially learning related to our professional success in the world—takes a long time. But it doesn't have to. When you get the right wisdom in the room, facilitated around your unique learning objectives, you can condense days, weeks, months, and I'm even going to say years, of learning, into hours.

Engage Your Operators

To craft conversations as powerful as those I had about doing business in China, the key is to set yourself up to participate as fully as possible, to truly engage with your operators in the limited time you have them on the phone. GXG helps our clients significantly with this part by always having a facilitator on the line—someone from the client fulfillment team who knows the client and their challenge well, and has also spent time getting to know the expert before we connect them.

But never fear! The beauty of the work you've done so far, defining your destination and mapping the ecosystem of your challenge is that you can simply focus on one learning gap, one person, one hour at a time.

To get started, I'm asking you to find a humble space once again. Take a candid, vulnerable look at the knowledge gap you hope to address on your call with a particular wise person. Try to narrow the scope of what you don't know, where your "flat side" is, as much as possible. For example, instead of asking "how do I manage team performance?" try "how do I implement OKRs for a mixed team of technical and business people?" Preparing questions like this will paint a much clearer picture for your expert, allowing them to jump right in with the most relevant and more detailed advice. Help them help you.

You can further maximize your time with this rock star you found by exchanging as much info as possible in advance. Send your bio, additional context on your problem, and your top three questions a day before. This is not only courteous, but it's a great forcing function to make sure you're super dialed in to the value you hope to extract. I'm aware that this is not mind-blowing advice. But remember that you are approaching people who likely have experience with other types of exploratory expert network calls. Maybe you've participated in some yourself! I accept them from time to time as a reality check—is what we offer clients really so different? I'm always reassured. In my experience, neither participant knows much about the other when the call starts and we spend the majority of the time dancing around trying to figure out where the value is. Without a third party facilitator to guide you, preparation and a little preliminary relationship building is your friend.

Finally, look for opportunities to reciprocate. I know earlier I emphasized that these relationships don't have to be strictly quid pro quo; generalized reciprocity means people are willing to give without a specific promise of return. However, that concept only works if you foster a genuine willingness to help someone else in turn. Spend some time thinking about where you might have a similar level of expertise to pay forward and put it out there. Conversation by conversation, you'll build a network of people with a few amazing things in common: a willingness to help others, wisdom around a specific set of business challenges, and you! There's no telling what else those relationships can spark over time if you're willing to activate them.

Building Better Outcomes

Just as I will never forget the start of my first one-hour conversation—I won't forget my reactions as the call ended. I was blown away at how much I had learned in just 60 minutes from a complete stranger.

After two or three more of these one-hour conversations with practitioner-advisors, I was astounded at how rapidly I was extending my network of people who were demonstrably helping me. None of this was generic conversation about the broad topics commonly floated at networking events. Every discussion was specifically tailored to my needs. I could feel my gaps being filled with useful information. The very specificity of these conversations focused and accelerated my learning.

The people I spoke with had strong, direct strong opinions. Try this. Don't do that. Have you talked to so-and-so? Those one-hour sessions sent me zooming me up the learning curve, and my skepticism melted away. Vetted, intensely customer focused one-hour conversations build relationships on intellectual steroids.

It's critical you don't let the rush of your first round of conversations mush together into more noise. You have to synthesize what you've learned into actionable steps.

One of GXG's clients is the head of a Fortune 500 financial services company who asked for help in closing a broad number of gaps, ranging from consumer behavior to digital technology and the best use of accumulated data. Having defined our targets, we took aim and found 14 longtime operators with experience in seven specific areas: business model transformation, digital engagement, digital intelligence, connectivity, consumer behavior, design thinking, and then corporate culture and talent. After recruiting the experts, GXG created the agenda for these conversations, providing all the relevant information to prepare participants for each discussion. The objective then became facilitating every dialogue to advance toward our desired outcomes.

This also required synthesizing the key takeaways from each connection and activating next steps from those connections to ensure that the knowledge acquired was put into productive action.

The outcomes?

- Growth levers: The CEO learned how his company could create better customer experiences and add new services to the portfolios the company's 15,000 advisors used in their daily work with customers.

- Business process optimization: The company began to leverage data and analytics to improve efficiency.

- Cultural transformation: The CEO's strongest new relationship was with a veteran operator we initially introduced. They took it from there and built specific initiatives that energized the company's entire staff in support of these innovations.

These were built piece by piece, one conversation at a time, by summarizing the key takeaways with the client at the end of every call. If you adopt this practice, I know you'll see exponential value in every additional call you have. One of the simplest ways to synthesize every call is to ask yourself afterward, "What am I going to do differently?" What wisdom did you hear that challenges the practices that have gotten and kept you stuck? It is about bringing in the knowledge you need, right here and right now, to get you moving in the right direction.

The Digital Advisory Board

We can't do things the way we have always done them and expect to survive. That's a real problem because most leaders think of change as an enemy. CEOs embrace the status quo and often will defend it to their death. In contrast, my passion is to find and develop agile leaders who I define primarily as seeing change as an opportunity they embrace. This can be terrifying if you are charged with the awesome responsibility of leading high-stakes enterprises on which the well-being of employees, investors, and customers depend.

Not surprisingly, we find that many leadership teams are stuck on some aspect of digital transformation, like I was at Assurant Solutions.

In many cases, this is a basic question of saving on cost and time through digital development while delivering a better, more competitive customer experience. But I remember coming back from a national conference on the future of digital development, astonished at a question the organizers asked the crowd: "How digitally ready is your organization from a cultural perspective?" The No. 1 answer that came back was: We expect to have parity with our competitors. Now, remember that this was a conference on the digital future, so the attendees presumably aspired to develop in this area. I could not believe that the No. 1 response essentially meant: "We aspire to be mediocre."

Remember the question I just taught you to ask after every connection call: "What am I going to do differently?" By aspiring to do things differently, I'm asking you to reach well beyond parity or mediocrity. Parity is slow. Mediocrity is stuck! That is the principle that unites the work I do with individual leaders, the process I am sharing with you, and wisdom-transfer environment of an advisory board.

At the very least, I was determined that we at Assurant Solutions would not be mediocre. That's why I agreed to let GXG to help us to organize a group of these knowledgeable, experienced people as a new kind of digital advisory board to work directly with my senior leadership team.

And that's why I'm so excited to bring wisdom-based learning to you, through this book, and to other leaders though GXG programs. The power of this wisdom-based learning is quite literally my professional passion. If you'll allow me, I'll sum up this fourth step—activate the wisdom—with one more anecdote.

Recently, I was talking with a Fortune 500 leader who said, "One of the most refreshing things about these conversations you coordinate for us is that I actually get to stop and listen to what is being said—even if it runs counter to what I had been thinking."

"That's unusual?" I asked.

"Certainly," he said. "You've seen how this works in a leadership team. If someone dares to bring up a contrary idea, a challenge or a tough question we didn't expect—there's this big temptation to cut them off. We feel like we can't waste time going down some other path. Over time, people learn not to bring up those challenges in the first place. In choosing these outside experts to bring to our table—you're intentionally building challenges into our conversations. You make us listen to ideas we might never have heard if were left on our own."

"I never thought about it in exactly those terms—but you're right. That's exactly our intention."

He looked at me directly and said, "That's one of the most valuable things you do. You make us stop and listen—really listen—to points of view that we might never let into the room, otherwise."

Step Four: Activate

Tips

- Prepare as much as you can for each conversation in advance by:
- exchanging bios ahead of time.
- providing any additional context on your work that might be helpful.
- sending over some initial questions.
- Try video conferencing! It's an easy way to ensure both of you are fully engaged in the conversation.
- Take hand written notes instead of typed. Research shows that typed notes focus too much on accuracy and not enough on conceptualization.
- Synthesize the conversation into two to three major topics, with bullet points, and one key takeaway.

Exercise

Try it! Pick one of your knowledge gaps from the end of Chapter 7 and do some research to identify an operator who seems to have the wisdom you need. Reach out!

Make It Happen

When you make it to this point in the process, and I know you'll make it, there's only one more step: Make it happen! Unfortunately, this is the step where I have the least amount of advice to share. What you need to do now depends so much on your challenge, your role, and your organization. You have to weigh what you heard from other wise operators and fit that into a path that makes sense for you. I only want to remind you that while you are out there, tackling your challenge step by step, the process you have learned here never has to stop. The best way to ensure that you get unstuck and stay unstuck is to keep making space for the knowledge and experience of others.

What I can leave you with is how the Assurant Solutions Digital Advisory Board (DAB) shaped the way we pursued our digital transformation. I remember the electricity that began to flow when our DAB formed and started to function. These really smart people were helping us embark on this complex journey from A to B as a realistic path that we all agreed to take. In one meeting, I said, "This feels like we're *de-risking* this whole new world."

We call this commitment to honesty and clarity "raising the guardrails," so that driving fast becomes a carefully calculated risk.

However, there is a big difference between daring and foolhardy.

In business, guardrails are built on foundations of honesty. As we have seen already, honesty is a crucial value in the process of humbly admitting that a leadership team is stuck on important issues. We also know that bringing in the wisdom of outside operators can increase the accuracy of our assessment of what is possible. These advisors have driven this course before us and can provide a crystal-clear preview of the twists and turns we are about to encounter. IF we are honest.

How Do We Raise the Guardrails?

Duke University's pioneering behavioral economist Dan Ariely has spent years researching honesty and dishonesty, including studies involving students at Harvard, MIT, and other top universities. Ariely's first conclusion about dishonesty certainly is not surprising to anyone who has spent much time in Fortune 500 companies: "When given the opportunity, many honest people will cheat."

It's his second conclusion that is so surprising. All it took to increase the level of honesty in his test groups was to remind participants of a basic, widely known moral code. In some experiments, his team asked participants to spend just a few minutes thinking about the Ten Commandments before they began the actual experiment. In another famous experiment, MIT students were told that their activity "falls under the MIT honor system." In reality, there is no such system. Nevertheless, the mere reminder of the Ten Commandments or an "honor system" reduced the group's overall dishonesty. In his book, *Predictably Irrational,* Ariely concludes that the rise in white-collar dishonesty we have seen in recent years is related to a widespread amnesia about what it means to be a professional. "The word profession comes from the Latin *professus,* meaning 'affirmed publicly'," Ariely tells readers.

In today's turbulent global economy, we can easily forget the simple truth that it is good to be honest. That's why leaders who have worked with our team over the years respond so positively to our team's reminders about honesty, a value that normally one might never think to mention. What Ariely's research has proven repeatedly is: We can't let this go without saying it aloud. In fact, Ariely's studies show that simply mentioning the value of honesty has a demonstrable and positive effect on the choices we make. It helps us to rethink the way we conduct business and adapt to the future.

At GXG, we describe this overall process as raising the guardrails—reminding everyone involved that we are not pushing reckless risks. Yes, we want to help leaders swiftly make crucial choices, but raising the guardrails involves careful attention to our deepest, most secure foundations. Raising the guardrails means that we welcome the wisdom of our senior leadership team, our best in-house research, our consultants' most valuable findings, and the warnings of our top advisors. We sift all of that information along with our new outside advisors—the operators who will help us chart the future.

The honesty produced in this process comes in three main forms: authenticity, accuracy, and clarity.

Authenticity

If we could, we would trademark "honesty" as a core GXG value, because it's so important. However, that doesn't mean honesty feels warm and fuzzy. The first form of honesty we practice is authenticity with our clients and with the operators who agree to help us. Look up that word. You'll find that authentic means "genuine, original, bona fide and true."

I have an example I like to use to really emphasize the kind of honesty I'm talking about. Think of a time when you met up with friends who had a new baby. We all tend to say the same thing: "what a beautiful baby!" But when we get in the car to go home, how many of us glance at our friend or spouse and admit the truth; "that was one ugly baby." Now the good news is that babies grow up, grow into their features, and everyone tends to turn out pretty great. We know this, so we don't remark on babies' giant heads or funny wrinkles or squished up faces. But in a stuck organization, we desperately need the sort of ridiculous, radical transparency it would take to tell someone their baby is ugly.

I can tell you from personal experience that an initial full-strength dose of authenticity hurts! When GXG first formed a digital advisory board for me at Assurant Solutions, our senior leadership team already was committed to driving this process as rapidly as we could. Both the global market and the technology were moving too fast to learn the old way, which is why we engaged in this new process. We thought we were ready to roar out onto that new racecourse.

We weren't. None of us who were involved in that first digital advisory board meeting will ever forget it. We staggered shell-shocked out of that first encounter with these new outside advisors. Their honest appraisal of where we stood, and how far we needed to go, had been brutal.

"Well, the good news is the people on this new advisory board are all smart people," I remember saying to my colleagues in the aftermath of that first meeting. "The bad news is they totally savaged us." In a respectful way, of course! But it still felt like they called our baby ugly.

I looked around the faces of my leadership team. I could tell they were on the verge of slinking away to nurse their wounds.

"Here's some more good news," I said. "This new advisory board has made it clear we are at an inflection point—if we choose to seize this opportunity. We have two paths here. We can mope around doing pretty much what we've already been doing—or we can fully engage in this process and really take to heart the wisdom this advisory board is offering. They want to help us become successful by learning how to do these very difficult new things. They showed up here because they believe we can do it. If we can push through the initial pain of this brutal assessment, then I know we can successfully drive this change through our whole organization. They think we can do it. I think we can do it. Are you with me?"

Heads were nodding. Several people said encouraging things.

"It will help all of us to think of this as an honest gut check," I said. "I'm confident we're a great team. What they said wasn't personal. They were just shining a laser light on the truth that our leadership team, right now, simply doesn't have the wisdom to do this new kind of work we need to do. Yes, it was brutal to hear that, but they were trying to show us where we can gain real traction if we accept the wisdom they are willing to share with us. They're really smart people, and they can help us figure out how to get where we want to go." It's critical to understand that they were not 'better' people. They were not harder workers or more dedicated. But they did have the wisdom to know they needed to be honest with us in order to help us move forward.

I got signs of encouragement from my team.

"Think of what just happened as the explosion we needed to get us past our inertia," I said. "Let's go do this together."

Then, the leadership team proved they were with me. We continued with the advisory board, and these outside operators showed us that they were right: This was an inflection point for Assurant Solutions. Starting with this tough initial engagement, then working together over the next two years, Assurant Solutions went from having pretty much no meaningful digital experience to becoming a digitally accomplished, savvy and competitive company. The proof of our success was our acceptance at the table by iconic digital organizations, including Amazon, Google and eBay. Less than twelve months before it was unimaginable that we would do business with these types of digitally savvy companies.

Accuracy

As we worked with the advisory board, we soon agreed on the second valuable facet of honesty: accuracy. While trust is built on authentic relationships, we also need to rigorously pursue the truth. Accuracy wins.

In May 2019, *The New York Times* profiled a "revolutionary" competitor who proved the truth of that assertion. *The Times* wrote: "Instead of viewing him as a mere contestant, we ought to think of him as one of that special breed of innovators who completely change the stage on which they perform." This wasn't a news story about a professional athlete; this was a jaw-dropping profile of James Holzhauer. He was winning so much money so fast on the game show *Jeopardy!* that reporters were saying that he had "broken the game" and might never be beaten. Of course, he was defeated in his 33rd appearance, after having racked up $2.46 million in winnings—just shy of Ken Jennings' record of $2.52 million in Ken's 75 appearances.

How did he win so much so fast? A lot of commentators focused on Holzhauer's intimidating stance while playing, coupled with his unorthodox style of starting at the bottom of the *Jeopardy!* game board with the highest-value clues. Those techniques did help him, but the truth is that Holzhauer won mainly because he was one of the most accurate contestants ever to play the game. A professional sports gambler, he understood that accuracy was the key to this competition. He devoted a year to studying likely topics, from geography to science and the fine arts. In his training, he relied heavily on books written and illustrated for schoolchildren to increase his odds at retaining their simpler presentation of the facts. In *Jeopardy!* the biggest risks are called Daily Doubles. Each time Holzhauer could find one of the hidden Daily Doubles on the big board, he would bet big—often shocking even the game's host, Alex Trebek, with the size of his wagers. Over time, Holzhauer made these bets with increasing confidence because his accuracy rate on those high-stakes clues was 94.7%. In his 33rd game, the one he finally lost to Chicago librarian Emma Boettcher, Holzhauer never gave an incorrect answer. She simply was faster at correctly responding to more high- value clues. In later media reports dissecting her big win, *Jeopardy!* viewers learned that her strategy also focused on accuracy. She had written her master's thesis on decoding the complexity of the game's thousands of clues. She was just as confident as he was in making big bets, because she had perfected her own rate of accuracy.

This may sound like a simple lesson: Accuracy wins. Yet it is astonishing to find the sloppy ways many leaders, and even business consultants who should know better, overlook the importance of accuracy as they try to raise the guardrails.

Here's an example known to millions: A very popular business video on YouTube features a leadership consultant from the U.K. who advises executives on how to prepare talks for large groups of people. One of his tips is to start with "a factoid that will shock the audience." He insists this is easy because Google can help to confirm the accuracy of such attention-getting factoids. Then, he recommends one of his most effective opening lines: "There are more people alive today than have ever lived." As he delivers this line, he pauses for dramatic effect, then he repeats the line again. His audience at a networking conference where the video was produced is suitably impressed as they ponder this mind-boggling idea. More than 10 million viewers have watched this video, so presumably lots of executives' stump speeches now are repeating this gee-whiz line.

The problem is: It's totally false! It's not even close to being accurate. This consultant brazenly insists he has checked this fact and knows it to be absolutely true. That claim about having checked his fact turns out to be sleight-of-hand reassurance, actually deflecting people from checking. If they do, a little Google research reveals that Arthur C. Clarke debunked that idea in his 1968 novel *2001: A Space Odyssey*. He wrote, "Behind every man now alive stand 30 ghosts, for that is the ratio by which the dead outnumber the living." More recently, reporters from the BBC News network revisited Clarke's novel and updated the demographic analysis. Today, given the rise in world population in the half a century since Clarke's novel, "there are 15 dead people for every living person," the BBC reported.

Just imagine having paid big bucks to attend that executive networking event captured in the video. You listened to that speaker—or watched his video later on YouTube—and then stood up in front of a major conference yourself and repeated that factoid. You would be risking your credibility as a leader on the chance that no one in your audience would actually check your thought-provoking opening line.

If anyone bothered to check, your reputation for accuracy would be dead.

Accuracy is a critical advantage that you gain from wisdom-based learning. The knowledge and experience of others can help narrow your focus so you can move faster toward a solution. But it's not reckless speed.

Clarity

The third aspect of honesty is clarity.

The quest for clarity is one of the major themes in *The Three Box Solution*. Attaining strategic clarity is a universal goal among successful leaders, author Vijay Govindarajan explains. Clarity is the holy grail of strategic decision-making. The problem is that leaders rarely are able to fully complete that quest. We describe those chasms that keep us from our goal as being stuck. In his book, Govindarajan's metaphor for being stuck is more like a foggy, trackless swamp. Leaders get lost, he writes, because they can discern only "weak signals" about the future. "As the term suggests, weak signals are hard to evaluate because they are incomplete, unsettled, and unclear," he writes.

We may use different terms to describe this crisis, but we agree. In our learning methodology, our goal is clarity. Why? Because the choices we make as leaders matter to thousands of people. We need to see clearly the risks ahead of us. We should be held accountable for the risks we take. If you have read this far, you are probably nodding your head as you read those lines, because they are a summary of all we have learned so far.

Business is risky. We must know what's at stake and stand accountable.

Recently, I arrived for the second meeting between an advisory board and a senior leadership team from a Fortune 500 company. Like my own team at Assurant Solutions—years ago working with our first digital advisory board—this company's executives had weathered the shock of the authentic assessment of their new advisors. Now, they were weighing the accuracy of the initial findings and were anxious about how much they could bet on the clarity this process was producing for them.

After I made a few introductory instructions, I opened the session to questions. Several of the executives expressed guarded optimism. After all, like I had done back at Assurant, their CEO had committed to this process and was encouraging them to participate. They had tasted the stinging truths they had heard in the first joint session. They were beginning to see the wisdom flow. They still were wrestling with that third facet of honesty. Were they reaching strategic clarity?

One man from the leadership team waved his hand to speak. I nodded in his direction and he let loose his anxiety: "I think there's one big thing we all need to remember and that's accountability. I am 100% on the line with the risks we are about to take. I can see the fires burning if we get this wrong. In fact, if we get this wrong, I won't be here next year. My wife and my kids and I will be packing up and most likely moving next year."

He paused. "When we met in the first session, we were asked why our company has not taken many risks. Well, the reason is: If we do get this right, then we're all heroes. Everything is great. But if we get this wrong—well, we're accountable. That makes it pretty scary to take these risks. We've just got to be as clear as possible about what we're planning to do."

He was absolutely right. This work is a high-wire profession without a net. When we do things right, we're all heroes. But if we get this wrong—then we have no future.

I'm always grateful to hear that our clients feel they can trust what we're telling them. Our honesty in building these relationships— authenticity, accuracy, and clarity—is a key differentiator in the work that we do in this new approach to consulting.

In that case study prepared in 2018 for The Conference Board by Carey Bongard, Assurant Solution's head of Global Talent Management and Development, she summarized what happened next:

> Assurant partnered with GXG to form an ecosystem of subject-matter experts who served as an advisory group to the leadership team, with the goal of rapidly transferring knowledge and expertise. The Digital Advisory Board (DAB) was created in 2014. Its seven external members brought expertise in areas such as digital strategy, digital marketing, predictive analytics, and mobile technologies. The remaining seven members came from the leadership ranks at Assurant, including CEO, COO, CIO, chief strategist, and head of HR.
>
> In the beginning, we didn't know what we needed. The DAB helped us learn a different way of thinking and a different pace of executing. The DAB's purpose was to expose Assurant's C-suite to digital business and its industry impacts and to help them think through the implications for the company's strategy, culture, and structure. External members not only

shared their expertise, they also acted as sounding boards, asked tough questions, and provided feedback. This ongoing engagement with an independent group of external experts enabled learning and change to happen much faster than it might have otherwise.

It shifted how we thought about ourselves as a digital business. It had a huge impact on our psyche and confidence. Assurant decided it wanted to participate in digital disruption, rather than have digital disruption done to it.

Assurant's head-on collision with the changing marketplace and eventual triumph is a story often told around the company. But it's a tale not only about Assurant. It captures the strategic imperative faced by many "digital immigrant" companies—i.e., large, long-established organizations—to equip themselves for rapid changes in the marketplace, technology, and competitive landscape.

The advisory board helped Assurant's digital team build a credible strategy, an organizational structure, get the appropriate funding, and hire the people we needed. The Assurant distribution model rapidly expanded from selling warranties in partnership mostly with traditional big-box, brick-and-mortar retailers to companies that did most or even all of their business online.

As the head of Assurant Solutions, my goal was to help push these changes throughout the entire company. The experience transformed the company from our senior leadership team to our operational personnel as well. Everybody was getting wiser. As our level of competency was transformed, so was our corporate culture.

How did we achieve such a rapid adoption at all levels? I made no secret about how our digital transformation had taken place. I brought the advisory board before the entire company. There was tremendous pride when the employees at all levels of the organization learned that the head of Microsoft Latin America was helping us develop our digital operations, that the CDO of TOMS Shoes was advising our team, and that the head of data analytics for Sabre was on board, as well.

The credibility and excitement started to build, and it was clear to everyone that a major new player was emerging in the digital space. For the first time in our history, that player was us.

I encouraged men and women across the broader organization. I said: "Together, we are getting really good at digital. There will be no more suffering with that old inferiority complex that set in when we first saw our competitors getting good at this. No more having to shrug your shoulders and say, 'Sorry, digital is just not what we do.' Now, we are becoming digital leaders ourselves."

A Question of Vocation

We are at the end of my story about wisdom-based learning and how W = K x E helps leaders to get unstuck. Throughout this story, I have pointed out that the goal of this approach is a successful future for all stakeholders, including employees and their families, stockholders, customers, and the larger world.

So, here is the last secret I want to share with you: No single element in this process is new. All of our individual principles are rooted in foundational values as old as the Bible. I describe the core of our process as "a question of vocation." It's the kind of question psalm writers asked thousands of years ago: What is the enduring value of the work that we do? Are we making a difference in the world?

We take seriously the truth of these values and then strategically weave them through every aspect of our work at GXG. Remember that skeptical question from a client that I mentioned earlier: "Let me get this straight. Another top professional wants to help me get unstuck? Why would they do that?"

The answer is: They offer their time because they want to live in a world where people generously help each other.

I've come up with a rather common sense litmus test for measuring whether our work at GXG is worth the pursuit. Whenever we meet to discuss challenges or the path ahead, I ask a three-word question: Is this fun?

As you can tell now, that is a very serious question.

Our team also has other ways of describing this concept of "fun." They talk about "surprise and delight," which is a very insightful phrase drawn from half a century of customer satisfaction research—or even simply "joy." Marie Kondo recently became one of the most influential people in the world by teaching people to reorganize their lives around things that "spark joy." There is absolutely nothing new in what Kondo is saying—except that millions of people are eager to hear her reminders about that timeless message.

Corporate Happiness

I think we forget sometimes that feelings like joy and happiness can exist in corporate life. But happiness is as key to our work in the wide world of business as it is in our home lives.

In 2011, the United Nations General Assembly invited leaders in more than 150 countries around the world to start measuring the "happiness" of their people. That global appeal led to the production of fascinating, data-packed research reports each year about the forces that can raise or lower levels of human happiness. All of these reports are available online, now.

"We live in an age of stark contradictions," the first annual report declared. "The world enjoys technologies of unimaginable sophistication; yet has at least one billion people without enough to eat each day." The researchers then described "soaring new heights of productivity through ongoing technological and organizational advance"—while, at the same time, the authors cited the huge number of people facing poverty, obesity, depression, and other ills of modern life. "These contradictions would not come as a shock to the greatest sages of humanity," the report says, listing great teachers of the ancient world.

I had to smile as I read that. These annual reports come from top research scientists who are underlining what I have always known about life's basic values. Certainly, it's true: Driving corporate revenue is a powerful, positive goal that can lift up the lives of employees, neighbors, suppliers, and customers around the world. But we need to produce more than dollars. That's why the Business Roundtable issued a fresh call to responsibility in 2019, a statement that begins: "Americans deserve an economy that allows each person to succeed through hard work and creativity and to lead a life of meaning and dignity."

I'm tapping into that sense of "meaning and dignity" when I ask my question: Is this fun? I am touching on truths that are part of a timeless, global chorus. For example, even papal teaching describes our larger vocation as "protecting human dignity." An ever-growing number of Fortune 500 leaders agree: This is good business. For decades now, marketers have tried to assess the feeling of well-being by trying to identify points of "surprise and delight." Now, the Business Roundtable's new open letter rests on this idea that companies must be a positive force in the world. In their annual reports, the United Nations researchers sum up this basic human need under the umbrella of "happiness," which is a marker of well-being that researchers seem better equipped to measure than the broader concept of "meaning and dignity." The consensus is overwhelming.

Just as I earlier described the recent growth in humility research, happiness research also is booming. Formative studies in this field date back to post-World War II research into consumer preferences— producing those early findings that shaped the idea of "surprise and delight." Then, in the 1990s, researchers began seriously digging into all aspects of what makes people feel good about their lives—using "happiness" as the overall term. The workplace training industry contributed to this effort, too. Just as there are now well-established scales that corporate interviewers can use to assess humility, there are also scales to measure happiness.

Several of the most widely used happiness scales were developed in the 1990s and new approaches are introduced all the time. One of the most popular methods, cited in the 2019 World Happiness Report, is called FaceReader. That's a software product from Netherlands-based Noldus. The system watches people's faces to detect a wide range of emotional responses, with happiness as the ideal at the top of the scale. Noldus claims its software is 93% accurate at reading a person's mood. Want to know if the people in your community are happy? Buy the

FaceReader system, set it up, and wait for the results. The data might surprise you.

Clearly, we now know a whole lot more than we once did about whether people are happy—or not.

Unstuck

That still leaves the bigger questions, starting with: What makes people happy? At GXG, we are betting our future on a couple of answers to this question. The innovations in our wisdom-based learning process rest on assumptions about the pain that arises within our organization is in the cycles of frustrating activity that are swirling around being stuck. We have seen, time and time again, that happiness rises when we help people to get unstuck.

Earlier, I described the generational shift toward increasing reciprocity, that desire to help others without expectation of an immediate payoff. The 2019 World Happiness Report includes this idea under the category "generosity," which the researchers say is "a clear marker for a sense of positive community engagement, and a central way that humans connect with each other."

When are people most likely to be generous? The researchers conclude, "People are more likely to derive happiness from helping others when they feel free to choose whether or how to help, when they feel connected to the people they are helping, and when they can see how their help is making a difference."

That's what this model empowers you to do. Those authors could have been describing the nuts and bolts of this approach to making new connections between outside operators and stuck leadership teams.

What activities maximize happiness? Person-to-person interactions that form authentic relationships. The transformative power of this work are those catalytic conversations—real people talking and listening as they share their wisdom.

The 2019 World Happiness Report devotes an entire chapter to the correlation between isolation—especially increased "screen time"— and decreased happiness. In a chart that should be tacked up on every parent's wall at home, the authors list activities most closely correlated with "general happiness" among teenagers—our next generation. This is based on research led by psychologist Jean M. Twenge. No. 1 on the list of happiness-inducing activities is getting a good night's sleep, which will be no surprise to parents. Then, Twenge's team found quite a few other activities that promote happiness, including: sports or exercise, in-person social interaction, volunteer work, going to movies, and religious services. Most of these happy activities involve in-person contact with other people. All of the activities related to unhappiness were experienced when people are alone, adding to feelings of isolation. Most of these potential downers were screen-related, including video chat, texting, social media, and computer games. While this was a study of teens, the World Happiness authors make it clear that these findings underline a basic truth:

Happiness is often fueled through positive relationships with other people.

To that, we can say simply: Amen.

Step Five:
Make It Happen

Wisdom ➔ Confidence ➔ Flawless Execution

K x E

TO MAKE HARD
CHOICES

DELIVERING ON OUR OWN
EXPECTATIONS

I told you at the beginning of this book that I was giving you the punchline upfront. And I did! When you understand the wisdom formula, I believe you have a powerful lens through which to evaluate challenges in your work and your life. But I saved you a little something extra for the end.

Throughout this book I've given you a little to contemplate and a lot more for you to actually do. That's because our newly acquired wisdom is only powerful when it changes the way we execute. The beauty of wisdom is that it boosts our confidence and makes execution that much easier.

No more trudging toward that expectation line, unsure of what you're doing or how it will produce the desired results. When your targets are informed by the successes (and setbacks) of others, you are once again able to make choices with speed and clarity. The kinds of choices that you avoided while you were stuck. That renewed confidence allows us to reclaim our primary decision-making function as leaders and shepherd our teams through flawless execution of our initiatives.

Flawless execution? I know. I spent all that time at the beginning of the book talking about unrealistic expectations. But now you understand how to set your own expectations and some pressure-tested ways to meet them. The confidence you demonstrate through your newfound decisiveness spills over from leaders to teams, especially when you support their own wisdom-based learning. It empowers the talented people in your organization to get back to delivering results that matter.

This is what I really mean when I talk about flawless execution. We all want to make an impact in our roles. Wisdom helps us do it in new contexts and through even greater challenges.

In all honesty, I'm not a writer, and reliving some of my most challenging quarters as a leader, my most stuck moments, was uncomfortable for me. But I'm so passionate about the power of this simple formula (W = K x E) that I'll do whatever it takes to get it into the hands of leaders who are stuck and feel frustrated and alone. I hope that sharing my story will inspire you to take a chance on wisdom-based learning in your own life because I know incredible results are waiting if you do.

Your confidence will soar.

You will make the harder choices, faster.

You will know the thrill of flawless execution.

You will get unstuck.

Now go make it happen!

Now What?

If you're still feeling stuck or are curious about a more formal application of wisdom-based learning, please check out our work at www.GXG.co.

About the Author

Craig Lemasters, former CEO of a $5B Fortune 500 subsidiary, is an author, entrepreneur, investor, and board member with more than two decades of success in executive leadership positions, now dedicated to helping senior leaders get unstuck on the major growth challenges to their businesses.

When Craig took over Atlanta-based Assurant Solutions in 2005, it was a $2 billion purely domestic business focused almost entirely on a dying industry: Credit Insurance. Today, Assurant is a dynamic, high growth, digitally-astute global provider of protection products and other innovative digitally-focused risk management solutions.

Craig's insistence on candid conversations about knowledge gaps, leading by doing, and output-based strategies, reinvigorated the culture while laying the foundation for growth. During his tenure, Assurant Solutions expanded from a solely domestic B2B organization to include B2C offerings and a presence in 25 new markets around the world.

Craig continues to build on his leadership philosophy as CEO of GXG, an advisory firm that helps organizations de-risk and accelerate critical growth initiatives by connecting them with the right combination of external knowledge and experience. Craig speaks for a wide variety of industry and leadership audiences around the world with a focus on helping organizations more effectively navigate the journey from strategy to execution, a.k.a getting unstuck.

Resources

Ariely, Dan. *Predictably Irrational: The Hidden Forces That Shape Our Decisions*. New York: Harper, 2009.

Baker, Wayne. *All You Have to Do is Ask: How to Master the Most Important Skill for Success*. New York: Random House. 2020.

Collins, James C. *Good to Great: Why Some Companies Make the Leap ... and Others Don't*. New York: HarperBusiness, 2001.

Friedman, Thomas L. *Thank You for Being Late: An Optimist's Guide to Thriving in the Age of Accelerations*. New York: Farrar, Straus and Giroux, 2016.

George, William W. *True North: Discover Your Authentic Leadership*. San Francisco: Jossey-Bass, 2007.

Gladwell, Malcolm. *David and Goliath: Underdogs, Misfits, and the Art of Battling Giants*. New York: Little, Brown and Co., 2013.

Govindarajan, Vijay. *The Three Box Solution: A Strategy for Leading Innovation*. Boston: Harvard Business Review Press, 2016.

Grant, Adam M. *Give and Take: A Revolutionary Approach to Success*. New York: Viking, 2013.

Kanter, Rosabeth Moss. *Think Outside the Building: How Advanced Leaders Can Change the World One Smart Innovation at a Time*. New York: PublicAffairs, 2020.

Satell, Greg. *Mapping Innovation: A Playbook for Navigating a Disruptive Age*. New York: McGraw-Hill Eudcation, 2017.

Doug Stewart's TEDx talk, "5 1/2 mentors"

CPSIA information can be obtained
at www.ICGtesting.com
Printed in the USA
BVHW060238090920
588319BV00005B/122